(63-158688) 6-10-63

ULBRICHT

A Political Biography

ULBRICHT

A POLITICAL BIOGRAPHY

Carola Stern

FREDERICK A. PRAEGER, *Publishers*
New York • Washington • London

FREDERICK A. PRAEGER, *Publishers*
111 Fourth Avenue, New York 3, N.Y., U.S.A.
77–79 Charlotte Street, London W.1, England

First published in Germany, under the title
Ulbricht: Eine politische Biographie,
by Kiepenheuer & Witsch, Cologne and Berlin.

Translated and adapted for the
English-language edition by Abe Farbstein.

Published in the United States of America in 1965
by Frederick A. Praeger, Inc., Publishers

Library of Congress Catalog Card Number: 65–15644

Printed in the United States of America

This book is No. 151 in the series of
Praeger Publications in Russian History and World Communism

Preface

Is Walter Ulbricht worth a biography? His life is devoid
of great passions or petty vices. He is dull, compared to other
dictators; he lacks Stalin's demonism, Hitler's hysteria, or
Khrushchev's earthiness. Most of the time, he did not even
originate the policies he carried out. For many years, I have
read his speeches and articles, discussed his politics with
others, and always come to the same conclusion: As that merci-
less Viennese critic, Karl Kraus, would have written, "I can't
think of a thing to say about him."

But then why this book? Ulbricht forced his way into German history as Stalin's deputy, as Communist Party leader
and Chairman of the Council of State in the German Democratic Republic. And today, he helps to shape the destiny of
the German people. Yet people know little about him, or they
are misinformed. This ignorance about Ulbricht, and the
primitive questions to which it gives rise, could perhaps be
eliminated; perhaps we could alter our somewhat oversimpli-
fied notions of the man. These were my main reasons for writing this book.

There was another reason. The history of German Communism is—with some exceptions—being written today in
East Berlin, and being taught, with all the resulting falsifications, to school children all over East Germany. But is there

v

any reason why we should surrender this part of modern German history to the bureaucrats of the Socialist Unity Party?

The reader will note that I have not touched on certain matters about which Ulbricht is often criticized, while I have attempted to refute others. On the basis of the materials available to me, I have remained unconvinced that Ulbricht bears the guilt for Thälmann's imprisonment or that he blocked Thälmann's transfer to the Soviet Union during the time of the German-Soviet Nonaggression Pact. Nor am I of the opinion that Ulbricht primarily is to blame for the fate of those German Communists who died during the Soviet purges of 1936–38. We must be careful not to fall into the trap of a reverse "personality cult." If Ulbricht alone is responsible for the crimes committed in Germany in the name of Communism, are all other Communists, ex-Communists, fellow-travellers, etc., innocent? It simply is not so.

Since the end of World War II, Ulbricht's life has been so closely interwoven with his Party and with D.D.R. politics that it would have been easy to turn his biography into a history of both. I have decided rather to include only as much of SED and D.D.R. history as was absolutely necessary, since a rich literature already exists on these other subjects.

I would like to make a few comments about the difficulties encountered in collecting and evaluating the material for this book. There are gaps in the available material on Ulbricht's life, but I could do little to fill them. To appraise what I had was difficult enough: The volumes of Ulbricht's speeches and articles that have been published in East Berlin thus far are edited with a political eye; articles are missing that Ulbricht would like forgotten—for example, those in which he equates Nazis and Social Democrats, hails the terrible Soviet purges, or praises Stalin to the sky. Fortunately, however, the newspapers and magazines in which they originally appeared are preserved in Western archives. In the course of my research, I was also able to establish that many of the speeches and articles that *are* included in these East Berlin editions have been "abridged" or "revised" without comment. Such falsifications created additional labors for me, but I must confess I was almost happy when I could verify the original texts, firmly fixed in black and white. Once a text has been printed, it can be interpreted as you please, but it cannot be changed. Still, what I read presented me with many serious problems.

In doing research on the life of any man, one realizes that objectivity toward historical material is virtually nonexistent. Every biographer confronts this problem. It is not only party loyalty, concern for one's future, fear, affection, or respect that may cloud a person's memory, but also hatred—in the case of those who knew Ulbricht, a hatred that is perhaps understandable. Obviously, I read reports by today's East German officials with great distrust of their reliability and verity, but it was also impossible in many cases to believe what West Germans said. Considering everything Ulbricht must answer for since 1945, it is hard for any German who knew him in the past (and perhaps even fled from him) to search his own memory dispassionately.

The reader will find that I have omitted the names of some men and women who are quoted in the book. I did this at their request. Many persons whom I approached were unwilling to speak of their experiences or give information at all—mainly because they feared reprisals against themselves or against their relatives in East Germany. Naturally, I understood the need for caution, although in some cases their concern seemed somewhat exaggerated. This in no way diminishes my gratitude to all those who did tell me or others what they knew and remembered.

I should also like to express my gratitude to the directors and staff of the archives where I did much of the research for this work. I discovered important material in the Sozialarchiv at Zurich, which contains a collection of old Communist newspapers and magazines; in the Archives for All-German Affairs at Bonn, and the files of the German Social Democratic Party at Bonn. The editors of *Stern* magazine were kind enough to let me sift through the material they had gathered for a series of articles on Ulbricht. Ursula Alex and Gisela Rausch were helpful in compiling Ulbricht's speeches and articles from East German publications and in checking the quotations from them.

I would especially like to thank my friends Ilse Spittmann, Dr. Peter Bender, Wilhelm Pferdekamp, and, most of all, Heinz Zöger. They read various drafts of individual chapters, made suggestions both as to content and style, and always found time to discuss the book with me.

C.S.

Cologne
June, 1964

Preface to the American Edition

In his essay "The Practice of Biography," Harold Nicolson speaks of three principles that no serious biographer can ignore. "A biography," he says, "must be 'history,' in the sense that it must be accurate and depict a person in relation to his times. It must describe an 'individual' with all the gradations of human character and not merely present a type of virtue or of vice. And it must be composed as a 'branch of literature,' in that it must be written in grammatical English and with an adequate feeling for style."

I have tried very hard to do justice particularly to the first principle laid down by Nicolson, because I am concerned that the history of German Communism is being recorded today primarily in East Berlin—and that it is being falsified. True, in the West, a handful of scientific works on certain aspects of KPD policy have appeared, including Ruth Fischer's somewhat subjective opus *Stalin and German Communism,* but there is no over-all presentation of the history of the KPD and SED. For example, much too little is known about the ruinous role the KPD played in the last years of the Weimar Republic and how, by its fatal opposition to the alleged "main enemy," German Social Democracy, it unwittingly contributed to Hitler's victory. Similarly, little is known about the life and the political battles among German Communist *émigrés* in the years 1933–45, or about the attitude of the surviving KPD leaders during the Great Soviet Purge and during the German-Soviet Pact.

After 1945, we Germans, to a certain extent as direct participants but in any event as directly involved persons, witnessed for the second time (although under completely different conditions than the first) how totalitarian rule is established; the differing techniques (as, for example, that of deluding the people) used along with naked force to eliminate dissenters and win over the ignorant; what means are used by a certain faction of the official party to gain power and to silence the opposition within its own ranks. In short, we have witnessed "how it has been done and how it is being done." That is why I was concerned that this biography contribute to German contemporary history—Ulbricht and his rise to power constitute a chapter in German contemporary history, albeit a sad one.

I would like to add a few words on Nicolson's second principle, the depiction of the individual who is the "hero." I want to tear off the mask that his followers and official biographers in East Berlin have created, according to which he, as "the good father of his country," is supposed to embody "the best traditions of the German working-class movement." Ulbricht is none of that. But neither is he that devil and archscoundrel that some writers in the West have portrayed; one is liable to get the impression from their descriptions that they are searching for a whipping boy on whom to pin responsibility for all the evils of postwar German history. Behind the hero's mask created by the handful of Ulbricht's friends, behind the devil's mask created by Ulbricht's many enemies, is the ordinary face of a politically dangerous and spiritually warped German petty-bourgeois who has been helped to undeserved power by the upheavals of this century. How such a man could become the first citizen of a so-called German Democratic Republic, how it came about that he survived so much and outlived so many is told in this book.

C. S.

Cologne
February, 1965

Contents

ULBRICHT

I

"Let man be noble, helpful, and good."
—JOHANN WOLFGANG VON GOETHE

The Young Marxist (1893—1918)

Childhood and Adolescence

Leipzig—an old German trading center—was bombed thirteen times during World War II. The worst raid occurred in the small hours of the morning of December 4, 1943, when four hundred British bombers razed a large part of the main business section and almost all of the booksellers' district. A 79-year-old tailor was one of the badly wounded victims found among the ruins. He died three weeks later in a Leipzig hospital. He died alone, for his wife had died many years earlier. His only daughter lived in Hamburg; his younger son had long since emigrated to the United States; his older son was in the Soviet Union. When this older son returned to Germany in 1945, he ordered a tombstone erected for his parents with an inscription, LET MAN BE NOBLE, HELPFUL, AND GOOD, carved on it. Goethe's dictum may have been a fitting epitaph for the parents; as for the son—his name was Walter Ulbricht.

Walter Ulbricht was born in Leipzig, a city Goethe called Little Paris. It has an impressive cultural tradition: Leibniz and Richard Wagner were born there; Lessing, Klopstock, and Goethe studied there; Johann Sebastian Bach was organist and choirmaster there; and Felix Mendelssohn-Bartholdy conducted its renowned Gewandhaus Orchestra.

But Leipzig has another aspect—as an industrial city of steel and iron works, as a manufacturing city of agricultural machinery and mining equipment, as a shipping center. The nearby coal fields, its central location, the fact that Leipzig was a well-known trade center famous for its fairs—all these factors had contributed to its expansion. During the nineteenth century, Leipzig became one of central Germany's chief industrial cities: By 1875, there were 4,500 factories employing 25,000 people in the city; between 1870 and 1900, Leipzig's population increased from 102,000 to more than 450,000.

It was this Leipzig that became the "cradle of the German labor movement." In 1863, Ferdinand Lassalle and his followers founded the Allgemeine Deutsche Arbeiterverein (General Union of German Workers) in a Leipzig ballroom. Soon after, August Bebel and Wilhelm Liebknecht took the first steps toward founding the German Social Democratic Party (SPD) with the support of Leipzig's Workers' Educational Association. A few years later, Franz Mehring began publishing the Social Democratic *Leipziger Volkszeitung* (*Leipzig People's News*), whose wide circle of readers extended far beyond Saxony. From time to time, Rosa Luxemburg served as one of its editors. In 1890, after the anti-

Socialist law had been rescinded and the Social Democratic Party restored to legality, its strong Leipzig branch soon became known for its radicalism and Marxist revolutionary zeal. The tailor Ernst Ulbricht was a loyal SPD member who had helped to keep the organization together during its period of illegality.* He lived with his wife and three children in a cramped, squalid apartment; it was a life of want and misery from which there was no escape. Beyond these general facts, we know little of Walter Ulbricht's parents. We know they became Social Democrats, but not exactly when and why. The official Ulbricht biographies, of course, follow the usual propaganda line: The Ulbrichts were class-conscious Socialists who raised their children in the Marxist spirit.[1] But Ernst Ulbricht's daughter adds a human touch. She describes her father as a kind of amateur naturalist who took his family hiking every Sunday, identifying every tree and bird along the way.[2] Old Leipzig residents remember him as a thinnish man with a brush mustache, friendly and outgoing. He attended party meetings regularly but never opened his mouth during official business, coming alive only when the agenda was done with and "socializing" began. We are told that he liked to drink. After a drop too many, he turned quarrelsome and had to be taken home by his daughter, who would be

* Most of the laws restricting the right of association that were enacted in the German states in the mid-nineteenth century also barred political groups from establishing organizational links with each other. The Social Democratic Party tried to evade this ban by establishing a *Vertrauensleute* system. These *Vertrauensleute* (trustees) acted as the link between the members and the Party leaders. Since their relations with the members, leaders, and each other were ostensibly only personal, the police had no legal basis to act against them. Ernst Ulbricht served as one of the *Vertrauensleute*. See Dieter Fricke, *Zur Organisation und Tätigkeit der deutschen Arbeiterbewegung, 1890–1914 (Organization and Activity of the German Workers' Movement, 1890–1914)* (Leipzig: VEB Verlag Enzyklopädie, 1962).

waiting for him outside the meeting hall. (Of course, we must remember that these stories may be unconsciously inspired by the narrators' hatred of old Ulbricht's all-too-sober son.)

Perhaps, as a young man, Ernst Ulbricht, whose own father had been a laborer, had dreamed of owning an elegant and successful dress shop—but it was a dream that was bound to fail. Ulbricht could not compete against the rapidly developing ready-to-wear garment industry; instead, he found himself doing piece work for the larger manufacturers. He was doomed to do this for most of his life with no chance of improving his lot. Perhaps the question "Why don't I have a chance?" drove him into Socialist ranks, for the Socialists had an answer to that question straight from Karl Marx: The steadily growing concentration of capital, they said, was forcing independent artisans and small businessmen deeper and deeper into the proletariat because they could not compete with the capitalists. The rich would go on getting richer, the poor poorer. Did not the tailor have personal proof that these statements were true? Here was an explanation at last! In the party that gave him this explanation, Ulbricht found men who rejected emperor and church, opposed capitalism, and stanchly believed in a Socialist revolution—in a just world, if not for themselves, then for their sons and grandsons.

Ulbricht played no leading role in his party or his union; he was one of those tireless rank and filers who are always ready to take on small jobs like collecting dues or distributing leaflets, but he had no political ambitions. Still, the picture hanging in his living room was that of August Bebel, not the emperor; he celebrated May Day, not the emperor's birthday. His wife, Pauline, the daughter of a poor combmaker named Rothe, also belonged to the SPD, and she, too, had left the church. She worked as long as her health—which was never good—allowed, but her gout steadily worsened, and eventually she ran her household from a bed in the kitchen.

Obviously, these parents could not give their children much intellectual stimulation, but their political views undoubtedly left their mark. Fellow Socialists would drop in to discuss party affairs, and the children would listen; they even helped their father distribute leaflets, and, when they were old enough, he took them along to political meetings and demonstrations. After his school day was over, Walter Ulbricht would often read the *Leipziger Volkszeitung* to his father while he worked. Inevitably, the Ulbricht children became Socialists.

Walter, the oldest, started school first. The parents of some of his schoolmates also belonged to the SPD, and he and his friends spent their afternoons preparing to join the Socialist youth group. Fellow students called them "Reds."

It was not an easy life, being the child of poor people, a "Red," and an atheist. Teachers and classmates looked down on him. But young Ulbricht was virtually an outcast among the other "Reds" in his class as well, because he and his parents lived in the Naundörfchen district, a maze of narrow, dirty houses teeming with pimps and prostitutes. "Decent" men did not visit Naundörfchen, or if they did, it was surreptitiously. Self-respecting people looked down their noses at the unfortunates who lived there; as for letting their children play with a child from Naundörfchen, that was out of the question. This self-righteousness was not confined to the staid bourgeoisie; it was shared by many a class-conscious Social Democrat.

A Leipziger who went to school with Ulbricht and now lives in West Germany has said: "Ulbricht was pretty inconspicuous. He never said much, so we thought he was stupid. Besides, we didn't want to have anything to do with him. He lived in a neighborhood that was out of bounds for us. Ulbricht sat next to me in class for a while, but I soon forgot him."

Young Ulbricht was shy, not stupid. His quickness of mind was cloaked by timidity and touchiness; the surrounding hostility drove him deeper into himself. His official biographers claim that he read Darwin and Haeckel, both popular authors then, when he was only thirteen or fourteen years old. "We were all very diligent," Ulbricht's sister recalled later. "As children we worked hard at our school lessons. We never read trash at home, never. We only read the works of our classic writers, the truly noble and good."[3]

The same teacher who gave young Ulbricht these books is also supposed to have urged his parents to continue Ulbricht's schooling. But, of course, there was no money: After eight years in school, Walter left and was apprenticed to a cabinetmaker. At that time, he also joined the Workers' Gymnastic Association and the Young Workers' Educational Association. These clubs for young Socialists went in heavily for idealism. A Thuringian trade-unionist who joined the educational group at about the time Ulbricht did, has described its meetings:

> Our meetings had to be strictly nonpolitical and were supervised by the police. We discussed working hours, the evils of alcohol, and other important social problems. We were against exploitation, drinking, smoking, card-playing, soccer, and cheap novels. We were keen on labor history and wanted to imbibe culture. We took hikes in the country because a love of nature was part of our program. When we couldn't get a speaker for our meetings, we read stories and poems out loud. We read a lot—we must have been among the best customers

of the free Socialist library. Once, in January, 1908, Georg Schumann spoke on the subject "Why Are There Poor and Rich?" He used the bees as an example, describing how they simply chased the drones from the hive. At that point in his speech, the policeman monitoring the meeting leaped to his feet, declared the meeting a political one, and closed it.

On Sundays, the members of the Young Workers' Educational Association went hiking, with red handkerchiefs tied to their walking sticks, singing Socialist marching songs. Then, there were the "evenings devoted to the battle against literary trash," at which the boys, mostly apprentices, set fire to cheap novels. They went to museums, exhibitions, and plays, arranged literary evenings devoted to the classical German poets. Those interested in politics—Ulbricht among them—also read Marx, Engels, and Bebel. Ulbricht also enjoyed the workouts at the "Eiche" (Oak) gymnastic club. (As a boy he was always active in sports, a habit he continued to cultivate in his old age.) The young athletes also met regularly in the Socialist Leipziger Volkshaus (People's House) to practice calisthenics and to rehearse for club parties, at which they liked to present so-called living statues —"three-dimensional compositions under colored lights."

Considering his ten-hour working day, Ulbricht filled his free time with many activities. Beyond any doubt, thirst for knowledge, ambition, and diligence were important features in his make-up, but his official biographers, as usual, go too far in trying to make the present Chairman of East Germany's Council of State a shining example to young people. If we are to believe them, Walter Ulbricht also became an expert in these subjects: ancient, medieval, and modern history, architecture, stenography, political economy, literature, aviation history, pedagogy, geology, history of art, and the natural sciences—all this in the brief span of years between leaving school (1907) and entering the army (1915).[4]

In 1913, Ulbricht attended courses at the Leipzig Workers' Educational Institute, and this gave him a chance to display his talents as an essayist. Then barely twenty years old, he wrote a 74-page paper on "The History of Evolution in Nature and Society." Here is a sample from it:

> Two classes grimly confront each other: the capitalist class, approaching its end, and the proletariat, full of youthful vigor. While the proletariat owns nothing but its labor power, the bourgeoisie possesses the means of production. Economic evolution shows a tendency toward a rapid concentration of capital in a few hands, leading to an increase in the number of those who own nothing. The irreconcilable differences between the two classes, of which the causes are economic, grow increasingly sharper. The state is an instrument for preserving the common interests of the ruling classes. Therefore, the fight the proletariat must wage against the social order necessarily must be political.

Another essay, on "Political History," begins:

> If we study political history, we do so to gain a better insight into present conditions. History is the teacher of politicians. It is not that we can apply past history to contemporary events, but we can learn from it how present social conditions evolved. This study immediately brings us to the question: What are the driving forces of history?[5]

It must be admitted that these efforts hardly reflect the profound learning the young man supposedly had at his command. They do show, however, that he had already developed his dogmatic views and the dry style suited to them.

Wandering

In the old days, young German artisans used to spend a year or so "wandering" after finishing their apprenticeship. They traveled on foot through Germany or all over Europe, stopping and working at their trade here and there, and then moving on. These "journeymen artisans" play a romantic, sentimental role in German lore. Young Ulbricht, too, went on such a tour. He and two other boys went to Dresden in May, 1911, wandered through the hills of Saxony, and went on to Austria by way of Bohemia and Bavaria. From Innsbruck, in Austria, Ulbricht and one other companion continued on to Italy and Switzerland. Near Lucerne, Ulbricht took a job with a cabinetmaker and stayed through the winter. In the spring of 1912, he went on to Geneva and Zurich, then down the Rhine to Amsterdam and back to Germany.

One of Ulbricht's companions kept a record of their tour. Years later, the old man's eyes lit up as he recalled the "wonderful landscapes . . . the brilliant colors, the carefree life of those southern lands." For Ulbricht's impressions we must turn to his biographers, but they seem more interested in explaining how Ulbricht did *not* spend his time: He "did not wander along in carefree thoughtlessness . . . did not behave like the average apprentice" who "merely wanted to admire the wonders of the world." Walter Ulbricht evidently did nothing without a profound purpose. "His wanderings," we are told, "were part of his research plans." These researches—we are still in the realm of official biography—began at the hygiene exhibit in Dresden. There, the wandering youth concluded that "a really healthy way of life could not be achieved without radical social changes." He is said to have studied "the laws of beauty" in Munich's art galleries and have "felt a desire to delve scientifically into the meaning of art." He collected forty different rock specimens, "not because of their beautiful shapes and colors, but for scientific purposes." The dirty sheets at an Antwerp inn served as a glaring indictment of the capitalist system. Did the eighteen-year-old really see things this way or is it just part of the legend? Let us hope his walking tour was more lighthearted than his biographers would have it.[6]

Ulbricht joins the SPD

In 1912, at the age of nineteen, Walter Ulbricht joined the German Social Democratic Party. There were three factions within the powerful organization at that time: the Revisionists, led by Eduard Bernstein; the Centrists, headed by the party Chairman, August Bebel, and the great theoretician Karl Kautsky; and the Radical Left, whose spokesmen were Rosa Luxemburg and Karl Liebknecht.

More than a decade earlier, Bernstein had rejected dogmatic Marxism, denying that capitalist society was doomed to collapse. He wanted the SPD to concentrate on reform and pointed out that the workers had already vastly improved their lot through political and trade-union struggles. He insisted that the party must change from a Marxist-revolutionary to a democratic-socialist organization. Revisionism flourished in the SPD, although the party leaders officially rejected Bernstein's ideas and the orthodox Marxists fought bitterly against what they considered dangerous "bourgeoisification." Rosa Luxemburg wrote countless articles and several books condemning all attempts to "water down" the Marxist-revolutionary idea and advocating a proletarian revolution triggered by a general strike.

Most SPD members paid scant attention to the controversy

between the party's left and right wings, hardly suspecting that these theoretical differences would soon take on practical importance for each of them.

But the outbreak of World War I suddenly confronted every Social Democrat with the choice of Fatherland or Marxism. Carried along on the wave of patriotic fever, and seduced by the Kaiser's pronouncement "I know no parties, only Germans," many answered the call to arms. For them, the cry "Long live Social Democracy, International Liberator of the People!" had proved an empty slogan. Their nationalism was stronger than their international class solidarity. "We can truly say," said Eduard David, a leading Social Democrat, "that for us this war is a war of national defense. We are defending the opportunity to preserve the cultural level we have worked so hard to reach; we are fighting for the right to expand the living space our growing population requires in line with our economic activity." And the General Commission of German Trade Unions took up the cry: "Our enemies may as well abandon their hope that Germany will be defeated in this struggle; before that happens, they themselves will bleed to death and sink into the dust. Germany will emerge from this world war as the strongest nation."[7]

SPD leaders in the Reichstag were also ready to "rally round the flag in the hour of danger": They all voted for war credits. The Radical Left, hopelessly outnumbered, protested: "The time-honored call 'Proletarians of the world, unite!' has changed into the battle cry 'Proletarians of the world, cut each other's throats!' " Thus spoke Rosa Luxemburg. She, Liebknecht, and their followers attacked the SPD's policy of class truce as a betrayal of international Socialism. Their slogan was: "The main enemy is at home!"

Walter Ulbricht, too, had to choose between Marxism and Fatherland. His upbringing had been strictly pacifist and antimilitaristic; his party's leaders now seemed traitors to the sacred Socialist principles he had been taught in the youth groups of his native city. And so Ulbricht decided, in his very first choice between party and political orthodoxy, against the party. In the fall of 1914, Ulbricht joined a small group of young people inspired by Karl Liebknecht. His biographers report that he distributed anti-war leaflets and spoke at a meeting of SPD functionaries in Leipzig against the Socialist deputies who had voted for war credits.

In 1915, he was drafted into the German army. Stationed in Galicia, he wrote home: "The spirit of Prussian militarism systematically destroys one's character. The brutality here is indescribable. I am taking refuge in Homer's works and hope for better times to come."

In the spring of 1918, en route to the western front, Ulbricht jumped the train at Leipzig. He was quickly picked up and sentenced to two months' imprisonment by a Leipzig military court. After serving his sentence, he was sent to Belgium. In October, 1918, Ulbricht tried to desert again, and again he was caught. This time he managed to escape from military prison—at the time when the November Revolution broke out—and spent the last days of the war helping to form a workers' and soldiers' council. Then he made his way back to Leipzig. World War I was over, the Revolution had broken out. A new chapter in Ulbricht's life began: The young cabinetmaker joined the Communist Party and became a "professional revolutionary."

Ulbricht's Ideals

Sooner or later, when people discuss Ulbricht, they raise this question: "Does the man really believe in anything?" For most people tend to think of him as a cynic and opportunist whose every action is motivated solely by a thirst for power. This is wrong. Ulbricht believes in Marxism, the kind of narrow-gauge Marxism he learned at the turn of the century while serving his apprenticeship. It is the only kind of Marxism he understands, and it constitutes his one genuine contact with culture.

Skeptics may say that Ulbricht is much more of a Leninist than a Marxist. True, but Lenin's ideas comprise a theory of organization—the grand strategy by which Communism seizes power; they are not the kind of ideas that produce a pseudo-religious experience. Only Marxism gives point and substance to Lenin's grandiose tactics. Karl Marx is the high priest of Communism. But, of course, as is often the case with spiritual leaders, his words are open to many interpretations.

What did Marxism mean to the young Ulbricht? What does it mean to him today? For the twenty-year-old Ulbricht, Marxism was the key to the world. It gave meaning to life— something that most people, particularly when they are young, are searching for. Ulbricht was an eager young man, but he lacked the basic tools for thinking: stimulus, knowledge, education, and talent. Socialist educational institutions could offer him stimulus and more knowledge, and they also taught him how to apply his newly acquired learning. This ready-made attitude suited Ulbricht well for several reasons: His practical mind sought practical applications; he yearned for a way to express his Socialist leanings; he sought for explanations, and he took what was offered him. The uneducated youngster swallowed Marxist ideology whole, for the ideological fallacy propounded by his teachers, who equated Marxism with knowledge, satisfied all his needs. Here was a seemingly simple, convincing formula that enabled him to categorize and explain everything he learned, heard, and saw. Here was "truth"—the truth the ruling classes were bent on suppressing and keeping from the people. To be among those in the know undoubtedly gave him self-confidence and a feeling of superiority over his hostile environment.

Of course, thousands of others were trained in Marxist schools and did not become Ulbrichts. But then, Ulbricht had some rather exceptional qualities: his receptivity to "narrow-gauge Marxism," and a rather extraordinary discrepancy between aims and ability. Few men are as intent as he on cloaking their intellectual limitations and their inability to think independently under the mantle of "steadfastness" and "adherence to principles."

Once Ulbricht held this key to world events in his hands, he never let go. This is one of the reasons why he left the SPD and became a Communist. The Social Democrats would have forced him to test and retest his precious ideology, measure it against reality, and perhaps give it up altogether in the end. The Communists allowed or even forced him to hold firmly to his dogma. For the Communist Party would have lost its *raison d'être* without the Marxist philosophy of 1910.

Come what may, Ulbricht holds fast to his early beliefs: The proletarian revolution devours its children; Stalin makes a pact with Hitler; Churchill and Roosevelt make a pact with Stalin; living standards rise to unprecedented heights under capitalism; workers rebel against Communism; "capitalist" or "Communist" bombs threaten to destroy us all—but for Walter Ulbricht, the world still turns according to the same Marxist "laws" he studied fifty years ago. Small wonder that Ulbricht's enemies say he is pig-headed.

But with Ulbricht it is not merely a matter of adhering to the Marxism he learned as a youth. The older he gets, the more obvious it becomes that to him the spirit and outlook of the Young Workers' Educational Association represent the highest ideals to which mankind can aspire. If necessary, he will try to ram them down the throats of dissenters.

The Ten Commandments of Socialist morality that Ulbricht proclaimed in 1958 are part and parcel of this spirit: Thou shalt perform good deeds for Socialism because Socialism leads to a better life for all workers. Thou shalt strive to increase thine output, be economical, and uphold Socialist work discipline. Thou shalt lead a clean, decent life and respect thy family. . . .

The worship of the classics is also born of this spirit; Schiller and Goethe become pacesetters of Socialism; "decadence" in art is condemned. The "campaign against smoking and drinking," enthusiasm for sports—these belong to Ulbricht's moral and intellectual world as much as a dislike for new insights and independent thought. This terrifyingly simple world has no room for the individualist, the flabby-muscled, the hedonist, the Christian, the doubter, the bourgeois, the dreamer, or the artist.

II

The Apparatchik (1919–32)

Ulbricht Finds His Niche

Ulbricht was nearly thirty years old when he discovered
the instrument of power for which he had a real talent, an
instrument he instinctively knew how to use better than most
men: the *apparat*. The Communist Party gave him the chance
fully to develop this latent talent.

The German Communist Party (KPD) did not yet exist
when Ulbricht returned from the war in November, 1918.
Karl Liebknecht and Rosa Luxemburg, together with their
followers, called themselves Spartacists. They formed a small
group within the left-oriented, pacifist USPD (Independent
German Social Democratic Party), founded in the spring of
1917. (Led by Richard Lipinski, the Independent Social

Democrats had a majority in the new Leipzig revolutionary Workers' and Soldiers' Council.) Ulbricht joined the Spartakusbund and remained with it until the Communist Party was established.

He began as a volunteer propagandist for the Workers' and Soldiers' Council, visiting hospitals and attending meetings in his tattered army uniform, speaking for the proletarian revolution and an alliance with Soviet Russia. He was not very successful. The wounded soldiers listened apathetically to the young veteran with the odd, high-pitched voice lecturing them on the Causes of the Imperialist War and the Promise of the East. Nevertheless, Ulbricht was certain that the World Revolution was at hand. In 1919, for instance, when he addressed a Socialist youth group in Leipzig and found himself alongside another speaker from the USPD who told his young listeners that the revolutionary peak had passed, that the important thing now was for the working class to secure a solid foothold in the government by electing representatives and filling administrative posts, Ulbricht contradicted him, insisting that Germany was in a "Kerensky phase." In Russia, he argued, the Bolsheviks had swept away the Kerensky regime and the February Revolution of 1917 and had come to power. The revolutionary German proletariat would soon take power as well.

Ulbricht's comrades did not think too highly of his oratorical gifts. And Ulbricht himself soon discovered that he could better serve the revolution off the speaker's platform than on. His real talents lay elsewhere: He knew how to organize. Even before he had studied the principles of Communist organization down to the last detail, he was convinced that everything and anything could be organized—above all, that the proletarian revolution had to be thoroughly organized.

Did not Lenin, whose works he had begun to read, say precisely this?

In January, 1919, soon after the German Communist Party was founded in Berlin, the Leipzig Spartacists formed a Communist Party organization in their own city. Ulbricht took part in the founding meeting; by the end of the year he had become a member of the regional committee for central Germany. The Leipzig Party headquarters was a drab place with a few tables, an old typewriter, and some crates that served as chairs: The Party was poor, and most of its functionaries were unemployed; Ulbricht was no exception. He made himself useful at the city desk of the *Rote Kurier* (*Red Courier*) and later at the offices of the regional paper *Der Klassenkampf* (*The Class Struggle*).[1] For a time, he found work with a cabinetmaker, but his employer wanted no truck with a Communist and Ulbricht soon lost his job. He gave up cabinetmaking for good in 1919, and, until becoming a full-time Party functionary at the age of twenty-six, several months later, he made his living selling vegetables from a pushcart.

The Party left him little free time for working at his job. Leipzig was a seething political caldron in early 1919. On February 28, the Independent Social Democrats called a political general strike to force the government to socialize the economy and recognize the workers' councils. But the bourgeoisie retaliated with a lockout, and strike and counterstrike raged on until March 10. Even after the crisis had passed, the city did not remain quiet for long. In April, following the assassination of a Saxon government official named Neuring, all of Saxony was placed under martial law. The Leipzig USPD tried to obstruct every measure taken by the government and military forces, and as a result, the Socialist Minister of Defense in Berlin, Noske, ordered General

Maercker's troops into the city on May 12. General Maercker immediately banned the *Leipziger Volkszeitung,* the USPD's official organ, and the Communist press; prohibited all meetings of both left-wing parties; dissolved the workers' council; and arrested many Independent Socialists and Communists. Though Ulbricht was not arrested, he was put under surveillance. The Institute for German Military History in Potsdam has preserved a secret letter from the Leipzig Free Corps* to various military and political agencies. The letter, dated May 27, 1919, reads in part as follows:

> The Communist Walter Ulbricht . . . a contributor to the *Rote Fahne,* has frequently been seen in the company of the telephone operator Käte Reif at the Café Astoria (NW distr.). He is probably receiving information about military telephone conversations from her. Ulbricht is now in mufti, whereas before the military occupation of the city, he was always in uniform. Said individual must be kept under police observation. Unusual activities to be reported immediately to Corps Headquarters.

Ulbricht had more than one informant among the girls he had come to know when he lived in Naundörfchen. They had their own rather intimate connections with the occupation troops, and now and then were able to pass on scraps of information about planned anti-Communist measures. Because of these associations, the Leipzig morals squad began to suspect Ulbricht of being a pimp. After World War II, Leipzigers secretly called Naundörfchen "the goatee's village." Many a person who talked out of turn about Ulbricht's alleged past as a "bordello operator" and pimp fell into the hands of East Germany's secret police. So much for legends.

---

* The Free Corps were bands of volunteers commanded by regular army officers, originally recruited to defend the eastern borderlands.

Ulbricht's revolutionary activities in a *Threepenny Opera* setting take on ironic overtones in view of his known petty-bourgeois and puritan tendencies.

One year later, on March 13, 1920, right-wing radicals made their first ambitious attempt to overthrow the young German Republic's Social Democratic government and seize power. The government had to flee Berlin, and a right-wing paramilitary Free Corps group, the Ehrhardt Brigade, occupied the government buildings. Wolfgang Kapp, an East Prussian landowner and politician, placed himself at the head of a "counterrevolutionary" government, and General von Luttwitz took over command of the army.

The Communist leaders were the first to admit defeat at the hands of this new government. On March 14, the day after the *putsch* began, the *Rote Fahne* reported,

> Ebert [leader of the Social Democrats in 1919], Bauer, and Noske have mutely and unresistingly fallen into the grave they dug for themselves. . . . The revolutionary proletariat . . . will not lift a finger to save the murderers of Karl Liebknecht and Rosa Luxemburg from disgraceful defeat. We shall not lift a finger for this democratic republic which is nothing but a thinly disguised bourgeois dictatorship. . . . The democratic republic is a hopeless cause.

But the democratic republic was not a hopeless cause. The unions, the SPD, the USPD, and other political groups called a general strike in defense of the legitimate government, and government employees refused to take orders from Kapp. The strike made such a deep impression on the Communist leaders that they quickly changed their tune and, on March 15, called their own strike aimed at ending both the Kapp dictatorship *and* the democratic republic. They wanted a *Soviet* republic.

During the Kapp *putsch*, Ulbricht tried to help his party
as a supplier of weapons and information when, between
March 14 and 18, civil war engulfed Leipzig and three hundred people were killed. The Leipzig workers, assembled at
the Augustusplatz for a demonstration against the counterrevolution, were mowed down by Kapp's followers in a ma-
chine-gun ambush, barricades went up all over the city, and
the Socialists called a strike. The Leipzig Communists announced that they would join the SPD and USPD in the strike
if their demands were met, but fulfillment of the demands
would have brought a Soviet republic closer, and Lipinski
refused Communist help. Thereupon, the Communists formed
their own strike committee, of which Ulbricht was a member.
Johannes R. Becher, Ulbricht's official biographer, tells us
that Ulbricht commanded a "fighting sector" at a barricade
in the eastern part of the city.

On March 17, Kapp fled Berlin and the *putsch* collapsed.
The Independent Social Democrats called an end to the strike
in Leipzig, but some of the Communists, including Ulbricht,
thought the struggle should continue. The success of the
general strike had convinced them that the hour of the proletarian revolution was again at hand. The fact was, however,
that the strike had been strictly a Socialist and trade-union
affair. Except for a dwindling minority, the workers followed
the Social Democratic Party and other non-Communist
groups. The German Communist Party, with its 45,000
members and 589,000 votes (28 per cent of the electorate)
was still a minority political group.

The situation changed radically at the end of 1920, when
the Independent Social Democrats split over the question
whether they should join Lenin's Third International. The
left wing (and majority) of the USPD thought they should,
and did so in December. Thus strengthened, the Communists

again took the offensive. In March, 1921, a Communist uprising was staged in the industrial region of Mansfeld, near Halle and Merseburg, on orders from Moscow and from Party headquarters in Berlin. But the revolt was crushed in a few days, and a Communist call for a nationwide general strike went unheeded.

A few weeks after the abortive March uprising, the Communist leadership in Berlin gave Ulbricht his first paid Party job. He became district secretary in Thuringia and moved to Jena.

Johannes Becher tells us that his tireless activity and efficient working methods earned him the title of "Thuringia's Red Soul." But former Thuringian Communists now living in West Germany remember their one-time district secretary differently. They acknowledge that Ulbricht had industry and organizational skill, but point out that he was unpopular because he seemed so cold and withdrawn, adding that he was unsure of himself and subservient toward his superiors.

During his term as Thuringian district secretary, Ulbricht often had to go to Central Committee meetings in Berlin, and he attended his first Party Congress as a delegate in August, 1921. In November–December, 1922, he also went to the Fourth World Congress of the Communist International in Moscow and Petrograd as a member of the German delegation. But, contrary to present East German myth, on none of these occasions did he attract notice. He was still an unknown, minor functionary.

"Comrade Cell"

In 1923, however, Heinrich Brandler, then head of the German Communist Party (KPD), heard of the hard-working Thuringian Party secretary. Ulbricht, he was told, had brilliantly reorganized a completely run-down district in record time. Brandler was on the lookout for men who might be leadership material, so he went to Thuringia to interview the young man. Impressed by Ulbricht's enthusiastic agreement with his policies, and finding his comments on organizational problems extremely intelligent, he decided to promote him.

At the end of January, Ulbricht went to the Eighth KPD Congress in Leipzig, as delegate from Thuringia.* The leaders proposed him for the Central Committee, a body composed of twenty-one functionaries. Since he was still relatively unknown, Ulbricht was elected by only 112 out of 203 possible votes. Prominent Party members—such as Clara Zetkin, Hugo Eberlein, Fritz Heckert, Paul Frölich, Hermann Remmele, August Thalheimer, and Brandler himself—received more than 160 votes each. In a speech at the Congress,[2] Ulbricht identified himself as a "Brandlerite"—a follower of the ruling right-wing faction—and criticized the left-wing group led by Ruth Fischer, which had just been defeated.†

* In this account and in the following passages, I am indebted to the material provided in Ruth Fischer, *Stalin and German Communism* (Cambridge, Mass.: Harvard University Press, 1948), pp. 477 ff.

† The conflict between "right" and "left" Communists in 1923–24 centered mainly on their opposing views of the parliamentary and extra-parliamentary struggle. Another issue was the Communists' relation with the SPD, especially its left wing:

"The problem was brought up and heatedly discussed whether we could draw the SPD from its left-wing bourgeois position over to the right wing of the working class. We could then take advantage of bourgeois democracy in order to carry out correct working-class policies. The rightists among us thought the best way to do this was through a united front that would include not only Social Democratic workers ('united front from below'), but also special agreements with their Party leaders ('united front from above'), or, better still, a combination of both ('united front from below and above'). Brandler boldly said that the Communists should and would be on hand when the SPD leaders were finally forced

(At that time, Ernst Thälmann, who later became head of the KPD, was a member of this left wing. The leftists soon paid Ulbricht back in kind. When they returned to power a year later, Ulbricht was not re-elected to the Central Committee. His uninterrupted role in the top echelons of the KPD and its successor, the Socialist Unity Party [SED], dates back no further than 1927.)

Conspiracy was Ulbricht's main business in the summer and autumn of 1923, and he was perpetually on the go, leading the life of a typical professional revolutionary. He had moved to Berlin on becoming a Central Committee member, and from there he was sent to the Ruhr to confer with functionaries on resistance to the French occupation.[3] He also turned up in Thuringia again, where he gave advice to the local Communists. In July, 1923, he became a member of the Communist Party's new Military Council, whose job it was to prepare, under the guidance of Soviet officers, a new insurrection. Once again, Ulbricht procured arms and other military equipment. He also saw to it that weapon-parts stolen from factories and troop transports were properly assembled and distributed to working-class combat squads, mostly in Saxony and Thuringia. In September, 1923, when Zinoviev, Chairman of the Comintern, called the German Communist leaders to Moscow for a special conference, Ulbricht went along to report that every Thuringian worker was fully armed and had his own gun.

---

by a majority of their members to abandon their left-wing bourgeois position and join the right wing of the labor movement.

"The leftists warned against giving Communism a 'Western coloration.' To them, the SPD was simply a left wing of the bourgeoisie. An alliance with it would be treason against the working class. Its democratic illusions would infect the KPD. They fought only for the 'united front from below,' as a means of luring Social Democratic workers from the SPD." (Ossip K. Flechtheim, *Die KPD in der Weimarer Republik* [Offenbach, 1948], pp. 85–86.)

But just when everything was supposed to get going, it turned out that the Communists had miscalculated once again. On October 21, 1923, the congress of factory councils in Chemnitz withheld its expected support; Brandler had to call off the planned general strike and armed uprising. Only the Hamburg Communists, who did not learn of the change in plans until it was too late, plunged headlong into a hopeless fight that quickly ended in total defeat.

Ulbricht's enemies, especially former Party members and officials, have often pointed out that his success is primarily due to a well-developed sense of what is opportune, that he was always ready to betray political allies by switching to the winning side at the right moment—even if the winners were enemies he had only yesterday been fighting tooth and nail. Heinrich Brandler, the man who discovered Ulbricht and who was his first sponsor, describes how quickly his young protégé betrayed him. Brandler's enemies in the KPD and, more important, in Moscow, blamed him for the failure of the Communist uprising in the fall of 1923, and he had to relinquish Party leadership because of this failure. Ulbricht, however, immediately turned his back on Brandler and joined a so-called centrist group, that is, one that opposed both the right and the left wings in the Party. This is only one example of Ulbricht's opportunism, but opportunism alone does not completely explain his rise in the Party hierarchy. There is also his amazing skill at keeping *out* of factional battles.

The abortive Hamburg uprising marked the end of the KPD's postwar revolutionary period. Until April, 1924, the Party was outlawed, and even the most fanatical of its leaders had to admit that, for the time being, there was not the slightest chance of overthrowing the Weimar Republic and replacing it with a Soviet dictatorship.

It is hard for a revolutionary organization to hold on to

its members in such periods of disappointed hopes and crushed illusions. Day-to-day Party life, with its collection of dues and its long, dull meetings, lacks the romantic glamor of smuggling weapons and planning insurrection. The KPD lost more than half its members in those six months of illegality. Many of its officers were arrested, and Ulbricht, too, was on the list. A warrant for his arrest, made out in November, 1923, was not officially rescinded until 1928.[4] Forced to disappear from the political scene, Ulbricht did not return to public life until many years later. By that time, he had become an experienced, Moscow-trained specialist in Communist Party organization.

In February, 1924, a Russian Comintern representative, Manuilsky, came to Germany. Using the pseudonym Samuely, he rented several apartments in Berlin for himself and his aides. His job was to straighten out the German Communist Party organization from top to bottom. This "Samuely" had also been instructed to look around for suitable Party officials—men who could be trusted—to become obedient tools of Moscow. In Hamburg, Manuilsky found Ernst Thälmann, the future head of the KPD. In Berlin, he soon met Walter Ulbricht, whose position within the Party was, as it happened, precarious, to say the least. The Fischer-Maslow leftist faction had taken over the Party leadership in April, 1924. Not only had they blocked Ulbricht's re-election to the Central Committee, but they had also dissolved the "Cell Division" in which he had worked.* For all practical purposes, Ul-

---

* "With the Cell Division as our base, we conducted a determined struggle against the fateful anti-factory line of the ultra-left majority group in the Party leadership. The group around Ruth Fischer put an end to this 'opposition' by liquidating both the Trade Union and Cell Divisions. Comrade Walter was packed off to work abroad, and I was sent to Thuringia as political director of the district." (Franz Dahlem, "Warum er Genosse Zelle hiess" ["Why He Was Called 'Comrade Cell' "], *Beiträge zur Geschichte der deutschen Arbeiterbewegung* [an East German periodical], No. 2, 1963.)

bricht was now unemployed. Since there was a warrant out for his arrest, he could not very well look for a job outside the Party. Like Brandler before him, Manuilsky felt that Ulbricht had a special flair for organization. He decided to help the young man.

Traveling with a false passport furnished by his new sponsor, Ulbricht went to Moscow. There, for several months, he attended the Lenin School, a Comintern institution that trained Party functionaries from many different countries in Marxist-Leninist ideology, the Soviet line on current international problems, civil-war theory, and street warfare techniques. He was next assigned to the Organizational Division of the Comintern, and worked under the Russian Vassilyev in the Office of Cell Affairs. In September, the Comintern sent Ulbricht to Vienna as an adviser to the Communist Party there; from Vienna he went on to Prague in early 1925 in the same capacity. (To this day, nobody knows what Ulbricht's real job in Prague was. We only know that he met the men who after World War II became the Czech Communist leaders: Gottwald, Zapotocky, Smeral, and others.)

Ulbricht went to Vienna with a passport in the name of Stephan Subkowiak. As Subkowiak, a Potsdam draftman, he rented two rooms in different parts of the city, one for living quarters and one for conspiratorial work. For he had come to Austria's capital with a definite purpose.

One day before his arrival in Vienna, on September 11, the metalworkers had gone on strike. Austrian Communists were trying to influence this strike for their own purposes; they were aided in this effort by Comintern advisers—headed by the Bulgarian Georgi Dimitrov (later to gain fame for his role in the Reichstag fire trial)—and German Communist officials rushed to Vienna from Berlin. Their attempts to prolong the strike failed, however, and it lasted only one week.

On September 26, Ulbricht was to have addressed a meeting of Party functionaries on the subject of: "Reorganizing the Party: How to Start a Factory Newspaper." But on September 24, the Viennese police arrested him along with some other foreign Communists. Since the police had discovered his real identity, but not the extent of his political activity in Vienna, he was charged only with traveling on a false passport. At the end of 1924, after two and a half months in jail, he was expelled from Austria.[5]

Except for his short trip to Prague, Ulbricht spent the next few months in Moscow. While working in the Comintern's Organizational Division, he familiarized himself with the Russian Party's work in Moscow's large industrial plants. He met many foreign and Russian comrades at meetings and conferences. In March, 1925, when the Comintern invited Party officials from many countries to attend an organizational conference in Moscow, Ulbricht was already considered an expert on organizational matters, and his comrades nicknamed him "Comrade Cell." What exactly did this name imply?

The KPD organization, like that of the SPD, was based on local party groups. But this type of neighborhood organization was incompatible with Lenin's concept of the nature and tasks of a revolutionary party. He had held that the military and revolutionary character of the Party must also find expression in its organizational methods: Since the industrial workers were the shock troops of the proletarian revolution, the Party's chief activity must be concentrated in industrial plants; every factory must be transformed into a Communist stronghold directly responsible to the "general staff"—the Central Committee. In his twenty-one "Conditions of Affiliation to the Communist International" presented at the Comintern's Second World Congress (1920), Lenin had insisted that all Communist Parties follow the organizational pattern of the Soviet Party. They were to establish Communist cells in every factory.

The German Communist Party was, however, nowhere near realizing Lenin's principles. For one thing, the old Social Democratic ideas were still very much alive, and, for another, Rosa Luxemburg had always had reservations about Lenin's organizational doctrine. She had feared, and quite rightly, that such a military set-up would stifle every Communist's revolutionary initiative and sense of responsibility, that the Party would turn into an army barracks. Finally, postwar revolutionary upheavals in Germany had kept the German Communist leaders too busy to deal with basic organizational questions.

By 1924, however, the revolutionary tide had ebbed. Within the KPD, there were conflicting explanations as to why all attempts at Communist insurrection had failed. But the Russians thought they knew the reason for Communist failure in Germany: The KPD, they insisted, could succeed only if it were reshaped into a "new type" of Bolshevik Party on the model of the Communist Party of the Soviet Union. Reorganization by factory cells was one essential step.

Ulbricht was one of the few German Communists who believed in Lenin's organizational theory and was ready to apply it to the KPD. In 1923, he had specialized in building factory cells while working in the Cell Division of the Party *apparat*. At the time, he had written articles on the subject with such titles as "The Party Must Be Anchored in the Plants" and "Let Every Factory Be Our Fortress." His training in the Soviet Union strengthened his organizational ideas, and, in the years that followed, he maintained that the KPD's failures were due chiefly to the Social Democratic roots of its

organizational structure: "This organizational structure contradicted the Party's great task of struggling for a Soviet
dictatorship which is based on the factory. . . . The reorganization of Communist Parties on the basis of factory cells is
part of their Bolshevization."[6]

The KPD's new organizational specialist did not confine
himself to generalities. His real forte was detail work—devoted day-to-day attention to specific organizational problems
too tedious for the politicians. Ulbricht worked out minute
instructions on how to start a factory newspaper, how to distribute it, how to get workers to contribute articles, and hundreds of similar details of Communist organization. We get
a good idea of how his mind worked from an article he wrote
on neighborhood cells for Party members not employed in
industry:

> House-to-house agitation and propaganda play an important
> part in the neighborhood cell. Each comrade should be as-
> signed certain houses. Discussions with workers and their
> wives can be tied in with door-to-door selling of newspaper
> subscriptions and Party literature. Comrades whose jobs take
> them into the homes of workers, employees, and civil servants
> can easily carry on agitation. Casual encounters in stores and
> markets, at the barber, in restaurants and hallways, can also
> be used for propaganda purposes. It is important to talk to
> servants, janitors, etc., not only to enlighten them but also to
> get information about their employers. The neighborhood cell
> must support and guide work in local tenant associations,
> sports clubs, etc. Unemployment offices in the area of a neigh-
> borhood cell should be handled jointly with a factory cell. . . .
>
> The complicated, fragmented nature of neighborhood work
> requires an accurate listing of all sympathizers. Cell leaders
> must know precisely when and how each worker was ap-
> proached, where he works, what paper he reads, to what
> organizations he belongs, and how he lives.[7]

Besides changing Communist organization, Ulbricht and his Moscow masters wanted to tighten up the Party's working methods. They were bothered by the planless way in which the KPD operated. A handful of officials did most of the work while the rest of the members did nothing. How could this situation be remedied?

"Every factory," Ulbricht wrote, "has its production plan and work schedule. The Party's leaders must also work according to a definite plan," under which "specific people are assigned specific tasks to be fulfilled in a given period of time."[8] Such well-regulated working conditions required "strict centralism" and the elimination of all "federalist tendencies." The Central Committee would have to appoint inspectors to check on the lower echelons; all officials would have to be ready to apply disciplinary measures against comrades who were not willing to obey orders blindly.

Ulbricht's motto in the mid-1920's was "strict control and complete discipline,"[9] as he drew the picture of a German Communist Party based on the organizational principles of Lenin and Stalin. The articles he wrote then could be printed in any East German Party paper today; they are as pertinent now as they were forty years ago; the criticisms of the Party's failings and the recommended cures have not changed at all.

But in the 1920's, many German Communists fought this Bolshevization of the Party. They objected to the idea of setting up factory cells, since the big plants, they argued, had been cleansed of Communists, and the few Communist workers who had managed to remain undetected would risk dismissal if they became involved in cell activities. Another objection was that this division into tiny units—most factory cells had about ten members while the existing neighborhood branches had as many as a hundred each—would weaken the feeling of solidarity among the members and make it easy for the leaders to play them off against each other should any one of them rebel.

Their fears soon proved justified. The anti-Bolshevik opposition within the Party was routed and was never able again to hold its own against the new, Moscow-controlled leadership. In 1925, Moscow had put Ernst Thälmann, a Hamburg transport worker, into the top position of the KPD. Very popular with the German workers, Thälmann was nevertheless too weak to resist Soviet Russia's growing domination of the German Party. He was Moscow's spokesman and helped to further the Bolshevization of his Party.

District Secretary of Greater Berlin

In September, 1925, Ulbricht returned from Moscow to resume his work with the Organizational Division of the KPD's Central Committee. It was to take a few more years before he could leave the narrow field of organization and rise to "big-time" politics. In 1928, he was elected to the Reichstag, and in June, 1929, he succeeded Wilhelm Pieck as political director of the Party's Berlin-Brandenburg district—a key position in the Party hierarchy. Ulbricht was now the top man in the Berlin Party organization.

A few months before Ulbricht took on this job, Stalin had laid down a new line for Communist parties affiliated with the Comintern, proclaiming that the time for defensive action was over and that a new revolutionary phase had begun. The workers were to be rallied to Communism with the slogan "Class Against Class." Seizure of power was the immediate goal.

The world-wide depression—ushered in by the New York stock-market crash—seemed a ready-made opportunity for the Communists. Unemployment, it was thought, would radicalize the masses. And in Germany, the number of jobless rose from more than 3 million to more than 5 million during 1929–30. Every fifth able-bodied German was on relief; a father of two children received only 22 Reichsmark (about $5.30) a week in unemployment insurance. Right- and left-wing antigovernment parties grew by leaps and bounds. The German Communist Party doubled its membership.

Encouraged by this success and spurred on by Moscow, the Party renewed its campaign for the overthrow of democracy and the creation of a German Soviet Republic. On June 27, 1930, Ulbricht told the Reichstag, "With capitalism at its lowest ebb and totally disorganized, we believe the time has come . . . to mobilize the workers to strike against this system and abolish it once and for all. This is our clear and unequivocal answer to the question of how to overcome the present crisis." Six months later, in a Reichstag speech of February 5, 1931, Ulbricht ventured a prediction:

> The workers, led by the Communist Party, have struck against economic exploitation. In a few weeks, they will wage a political mass strike, again under Communist leadership . . . attacking the class enemy in his most vulnerable spot. . . .
>
> (*"Go ahead and get started!"—from the National Socialists.*)
>
> We shall tell the workers, there is only one way: They must be armed. . . .
>
> (*"Just get started!"—again from the Nazis.*)
>
> The German workers will get rid of their German and international oppressors only by fighting for a *Soviet Germany*: There is only one way the German worker can win bread, work, and freedom—by fighting for a Soviet Germany!

The new Berlin district secretary was now too busy organizing strikes, parades, and hunger marches to set up factory cells and newspapers. Jobless workers marched through the working-class districts in the northern and eastern sections of the city chanting:

> "Why, goddammit, is it that
> We're hungry and the rich grow fat?"

Street battles took place between the demonstrators and the police. But when the Communist shop stewards and union delegates came to the Party offices for concrete advice on how to help their desperate fellow workers, the revolutionary strategists all too often dismissed them with empty phrases: Two workers injured in a street fight in Neukölln? —A sign that the revolutionary wave is rising. The despairing wife of a worker has killed herself? —Let's make a note of that so Thälmann can use it in his next speech at the Sportspalast. The workers in a machine shop didn't get paid last Friday? —Comrades, all economic questions must be subordinated to the immediate need for mobilizing the workers against the danger of war, all Party organizations must concentrate on the planned antiwar demonstration. Mass layoffs expected in Weissensee? —Comrades, the *Soviet Union* is in danger!

Tenement children were begging their mothers for a crust of bread—the Communist leaders were feverishly absorbed in plans for defending the Soviet Union. "Illusions about the League of Nations and pacifism must be dispelled," Ulbricht wrote, "by stressing the inevitability of imperialist war and the need to defend the Soviet Union."[10] The important thing now, he continued, is to "spread the Bolshevik line in case of war; to bring about the defeat of our own government and the defection of imperialist troops to the Red Army; to defend the Soviet Union by supporting the Red Army; to turn the imperialist war into a civil war; and to establish a Soviet regime."[11]

This kind of propaganda suited the Nazis only too well. They knew that their own nationalistic demagoguery appealed to most Germans far more than a call to support the Red Army. In the Fourth Reichstag elections in May, 1928, only 12 National Socialist deputies had been elected. By 1930, things looked very different: True, there were 77 Communists in parliament, but the number of Nazis had jumped to 107. By June, 1932, Hitler's followers, with their 230 deputies, were the strongest party in the Reichstag. Democracy was in grave danger, and the KPD went right on trampling on it.

But, one might ask, were the Communists not intent on preventing the Nazis from coming to power? Priding themselves on their ability "scientifically to analyze" and "predict" political events thanks to their ideology, they had decided as early as 1930 that Germany already had a fascist government! No democratic parties had been outlawed, no concentration camps existed, Hitler and his Nazis had not yet taken over the government, Heinrich Brüning, a leader of the Catholic Center Party, was still Chancellor. But his emergency decrees, attempts to save democracy, were denounced by Walter Ulbricht in the Reichstag: "The Brüning government's way is the way to fascist dictatorial rule." On March 31, 1931, Ulbricht declared, "We Communists are the only ones fighting fascism, not only the fascism of Hitler and his minions, but also the fascist measures introduced by the Brüning dictatorship."

But to Communist leaders—in a period when the Nazi menace was looming larger and larger—the *real* enemy was neither Hitler's party nor the Brüning government: It was the Social Democrats.

As early as 1924, Stalin had stated that the Social Democrats were "the moderate wing of fascism."[12] In 1929 and the early 1930's, Ulbricht discovered that they were the "Social-

Fascist agents of Big Business," "servants of the fascist [Brüning] government," "forerunners of fascism," "bedfellows of the National Socialists," "the auxiliary police of fascism," and "mortal enemies of the working class." There was no difference between "Wels [Chairman of the SPD] and Goebbels, or between Severing [Social Democratic Minister of the Interior in Prussia] and Hitler."[13] The "most urgent task" was "to unmask the imperialist, Social-Fascist nature of Social Democratic policy." "In this hour," Ulbricht not only "exhorted the German workers, 'Down with Hindenburg and his policies!' but also, 'Down with Hindenburg–Social Democracy!' "[14]

On January 18, 1933, just twelve days before Hitler came to power, *Inprecor* reprinted a speech by Ulbricht in which he had maintained that "Now, as always, we must aim the main blow at . . . the Social Democrats. We must energetically resist every attempt to change Party strategy, every slackening in the fight against Social Democracy."[15] In a report made to Berlin district leaders at about the same time, he remarked that their chief task was to rid the working class of "Social-Fascism," if necessary with the help and support of the fascists.* Only then would the Communist Party be able to launch the final and victorious struggle against the Nazis. The Berlin Communist leaders acted accordingly.

In 1931, Nazis and other rightist groups organized a referendum against the Social Democratic government of Prussia. At first, the KPD branded this referendum as "fascist trickery," but orders came from Moscow to change the tune. Thälmann hesitated to carry out these Russian orders, but

---

* More than twenty years later, however, Ulbricht wrote, "It is time to examine scientifically our united-front policy from 1920 to 1932 and to decide whether the Stalinist formulation on the 'twin brothers' [fascists and Social Democrats], which hindered our collaboration with the SPD, was correct." (*Neues Deutschland,* August 1, 1956.)

Ulbricht and some others did not: The German Communists made common cause with the Nazis, joined the referendum, and now called it "the most radical declaration of war against the Social Democrats."[16]

A year later, the Nazis made an alliance with the KPD: This time, the Berlin Communist Party took the initiative. When the Berlin Municipal Transit System (BVG) moved to cut wages in November, 1932, the Communists called for a strike. But those voting for a strike in the BVG shop council fell short of a majority, and the unions refused to sanction it. The Communists led the workers out on strike nevertheless; Berlin's transit system was virtually paralyzed; and the Nazis joined the strike and took up collections for a strike fund when the unions failed to grant funds for strike-relief. Communist shop stewards in the transit system warned Ulbricht against this alliance, but the District Secretary would not listen to them. A few months earlier, during the election campaign in the summer of 1932, the Communists had made a point of their "irreconcilable hatred of fascism"; they had talked of ridding the workers' quarters of Berlin of the "swastika plague."[17] Now, Communists and Nazis stood side by side in these same quarters and rattled their collection boxes. "For the strike fund of the Revolutionary Trade-Union Opposition!" the Communists shouted. And the Nazis, "For the strike fund of the National Socialist Factory Cell Organization!"

The Communists defended this change of position as a "tactical maneuver." "Tactical reasons" also led them to adopt some of the Nazis' most effective slogans in the last years of the Weimar Republic. In August, 1930, the KPD Central Committee had published a "Program for the National and Social Liberation of the German People," in which members of the government and SPD leaders were called "agents of French and Polish imperialism" and accused of "repeated high treason." Like Goebbels, the Communist leaders "solemnly" promised that if they came to power, they would repudiate the "robber treaty of Versailles" and that they would not "recognize a single one of the boundaries" that had been "drawn without the consent of a genuine majority of the people."

The Communists also introduced a new, Nazi-like ritual at their mass meetings. Meetings now opened with martial music, flags, and fanfares. Members of the Communist veterans' organization stood at attention and formed an honor guard while the Party leaders marched in. The *Rote Fahne* reported one such Communist meeting in Berlin:

> Our flags burned red as blood in the setting sun. Their radiance filled all hearts with the firm belief that no power on earth could outlaw a Party so deeply rooted in the proletariat. This brilliant red proclaims the victorious idea of a revolutionary united front of the German proletariat. It says: "Berlin is Red and will stay Red!"[18]

Six months later, the swastika flew over Berlin and the German Communist Party was suppressed.

The Apparatchik

By the time Walter Ulbricht had climbed to the top of the Party hierarchy, he was a remarkably perfect example of a certain political type: the *apparatchik*. What, exactly, is an *apparatchik*? How does he differ from other types of political party officials? How does he come to power?

Even as a young Leipzig Communist, Walter Ulbricht was not very charming. He could not win friends—either for himself or for his cause. He lacked social graces, charm, persuasiveness, rhetorical gifts, originality, brilliance, education, imagination, and the vitality of the passionate revolutionary. He lacked style. He would not become a truly popular spokesman for he was unable to inspire the masses. He was simply not the type of man who came, saw, and conquered. So he had to work his way up through the machine and learn the trade of Party hack. His talents in this realm made him a useful Communist organizer. However, not every organizer is also an *apparatchik*. The Party needs and produces two types of organizers—the revolutionary and the bureaucrat. No revolution can succeed without the first, whose mixture of creative organization and inspired improvisation must be exercised daily and fanatically. Leon Trotsky was such a man. Without this master of revolutionary organization and improvisation, there would have been no October Revolution, and no Red Army.

The unimaginative bureaucrat, on the other hand, is out of place in an era of organized disorder and unpredictability. He must wait in the wings and bide his time. Guardians of order cut a ridiculous figure in any revolution. The bureaucrat, Communist or otherwise, is a guardian of order. But once the revolution is over, order must be established and maintained. It is then that the bureaucrat comes into his own. This happened in Russia, when a new state had to be built in the wake of revolution and civil war, when the revolutionaries had to come in from the streets and settle down behind desks. It happened in Germany, where orderly retreat followed in the wake of unsuccessful attempts at revolution. In Russia, newly won power had to be administered; in Germany, a group of discouraged though courageous revolutionaries had to be kept in line.

The unity of men in battle can quickly disintegrate in the humdrum routine that follows defeat—or even victory, for that matter. Not even the ideological robots of Communism can manufacture law and order instantly. Even Communist doctrine is open to different interpretations; there are many answers to how to rebuild the Party or why it has been defeated. Besides, there are always new jobs to be handed out after defeat or victory. Thus the groundwork is laid for the violent factional battles toward which frustrated revolutionaries turn for solace. This is where the bureaucrat comes in. It is he who assures the Party's continuity, for he has proved that he is both more able and more ruthless than the others.

Thus it came about that after the failure of the German revolution, thousands of frustrated rebels turned to the KPD and militated for action. The Party, however, has no use for men like these except in times of revolution or street fighting. But when the Party must lie back and wait for new opportunities, such activists are both a burden and a danger. They are enemies of continuity.

Nevertheless, for two important reasons, not even the rebel's opposite number—the ideologist—was able to assure the continuity of the KPD during its first thirteen years:

First: Many of those who joined the KPD did so after having made an earlier independent decision—to break with Social Democracy. As Social Democrats, however, these men had learned to draw their own conclusions and speak out. If the Communist Party really represented pure Marxism, then how much more important than ever before to think, say, and do what one believed! Soul-searching, conscientiousness, and independent thinking, however, when married to the new doctrine, inevitably pushed a new member into one of the many factions within the KPD. It immediately became his mission, therefore, to keep or push other factions—"wrong" or "misguided" Communists—out of power. Hence, a party that does not tolerate diversity of opinions or groups must guard against enthusiasts whose strong beliefs threaten its unity. Self-preservation will compel it rather to open its ranks to unprincipled opportunists.

Second: Many of these fanatical factionalists were well aware of the difference between German and Russian Communism. Even though they regarded the Soviet Union as the promised land, the first Socialist state, they rejected blind acceptance of Soviet Party practices and viewed subordination of German Communist policy to Russian interests as a betrayal of "proletarian internationalism." Many German Communists tried to resist the Comintern's transformation into an instrument of Moscow's—and ultimately Stalin's—power. But, split as they were into numerous small factions, their opposition remained ineffective. Like most of Stalin's foes inside the Russian Party, these factions yielded to temptation and formed temporary alliances with the ruling group in the Kremlin in order to suppress other factions. They were suppressed in turn.

With almost every new year, then, the enfeebled German Communist Party fell victim to a new disease. The virus of "deviationism" infected whole districts; members who were "healthy" one day fell prey to the dread disease the next. The various doctors consulted agreed at least on the needed cure: radical disinfection through expulsion or isolation of the germ carriers. Members who replaced the contaminated brethren did so for short periods only, since the healthy might fall ill tomorrow and the seemingly cured suffer a relapse.

The bureaucrat alone proved immune to deviationism. But it is not enough to ascribe his immunity and the strength he derived from it to the fact that the bureaucrat was nothing more than an apolitical opportunist. For what could the Communist Party offer a genuine opportunist under the Weimar Republic? Membership in the Communist Party meant sacrifice; there was the constant danger of losing one's job, of imprisonment. Had Ulbricht been an opportunist in the traditional sense, he would not have become a Social Democrat before 1918, or a Communist *after* 1918. He took both steps out of genuine political conviction. And even as a Communist *apparatchik,* he did not turn into a nihilistic cynic. On the contrary, the role of *apparatchik* seemed especially created for him to prove that belief and opportunism need not be mutually exclusive, but that they can sustain each other.

The *apparatchik* obeys the laws of the Party machine. The *apparat* is no place for visionaries; neither is it a place where programs of "general policies" are worked out. It is designed for detail work, for plodding. The *apparatchik* does not really care which of the warring factions is victorious—let others worry about these things—just as long as there is a winning political line that he can administer in an orderly manner. Not to know where to turn for authority is his greatest fear. He abhors factional struggles, with their continual change in leadership and their power crises. All he can do then is hold the *apparat* together. But give him a strong, entrenched leadership, and he can administer firmly and efficiently.

While a power struggle rages, the bureaucrat keeps as far away from it as he can. He avoids taking sides. He sticks to his paper work and, as soon as the battle is over, rushes to offer his services to the victor. It is of no concern to him whether the victor was once a deviationist, since all that matters is that the victor needs him. The *apparatchik* is a specialist, and he develops his talents best in a clear-cut power situation. He serves those best who need him most and who most appreciate his services. Opportunist? The *apparatchik* would emphatically reject the charge, just as any civil servant would who has served more than one government. He would point to his devotion to the cause. But what cause exactly? The *apparat?* The Party? Communism? For the *apparatchik,* the three are identical.

Ulbricht never demonstrated any clear-cut allegiance to any of the Communist factions that at various times were classified as deviationist. Ruth Fischer once said of him, "Every time he said something favorable about a faction he would qualify it—that later gave him a way out. Brandler? Yes, but now and then a little too far to the right. Fischer? Yes, only sometimes a little too far to the left." In the early years of the KPD, his lack of self-confidence may have been responsible for these vacillations. The bewildering variety of opinions may have confused him and led him to agree with the various would-be leaders in turn. But while others were fighting over "which line to take," he quietly straightened out the district in Thuringia and "thoroughly organized" it. "Ideological chatter" was not for him. His standard phrase, to which he resorted more and more often, was, "Today the question is . . ." He was fond of "asking concrete questions."

When he first got to know the Comintern apparatus in Moscow in 1924, he must have realized that the Soviets could use him and that the work they had to offer eminently suited him. Here he found everything he had ever wanted: tasks that transformed his failings—dryness, lack of imagination—into virtues. Here was a hierarchy in which the rules were made by others, while those who administered them could still enjoy high prestige. No wonder he decided for Moscow and, eventually, for Stalin! The apparatus able to transform a bureaucrat into an *apparatchik* was ready and waiting. Here was the center of power. What did it matter that this center lay outside his native Germany? Ulbricht was an internationalist, not a local patriot. Besides, as Moscow's man, he could stand above the factional squabbles of the German Communist Party, for none of the German factions offered him a satisfactory alternative to Moscow. There were at least two advantages in subordinating the KPD to the Kremlin: Power relations would be stable; and the *apparatchik* would have greater prestige and unlimited chances of advancement. Moscow needed disciplined and obedient administrators in the German section, not independent thinkers.

During the Weimar Republic, Ulbricht unfailingly represented Moscow's interests in the KPD. And, just as unfailingly, he helped to eliminate those who had other ideas. Even after he had risen from organizer of factory cells to Party leader of Berlin, even when he ranked fourth among Communist deputies in the Reichstag, he remained the obedient functionary. His comrades were none too fond of him. Thälmann, the swaggering man of the people, called him the "uhlan from Leipzig" and an incorrigible bureaucrat. But the bureaucrat had made himself indispensable. He knew and could handle the Party apparatus better than anyone else. And while men such as Schulte, Schubert, Schehr, and Lorin played politics, fighting each other tooth and nail to succeed Teddy,* the sober Ulbricht must have looked on with contempt, probably asking himself how a Bolshevik state could possibly be organized with men so utterly incapable of systematic work. Hitler and Stalin solved that problem for him.

* "Teddy" was Thälmann's nickname in the KPD.

III

When the Abbé Sieyès was asked what
he had done during the Terror, he answered, "I survived."

The Survivor
(1933—45)

Underground

Walter Ulbricht, Communist district secretary for Berlin,
addressing the German Reichstag on February 5, 1931: "If
this Chamber does not permit that someone like Mr. Goebbels
be described as he deserves to be, we'll have to do so elsewhere, and we'll use more than just words to teach [the
National Socialists] a lesson they'll never forget." (*Applause
from the far left.*)

Joseph Goebbels, National Socialist district leader for
Berlin: "We are going to make the gentlemen of Karl Liebknecht Haus [Communist headquarters] dance to a brand
new tune!" (*Applause from the far right.*)

But it was the Communists, not the Nazis, who were taught

a bitter lesson, for the Nazis made good their threat on the night of February 27, 1933. That was the night the benches, the speaker's podium, and the elaborate panels and woodwork of the German Reichstag went up in flames, while unsuspecting Communist leaders sat in a tavern discussing their plans for the coming election. The Nazi high command used the Reichstag Fire as a pretext for crushing the KPD. During the night of the fire, thousands of Communists were arrested, including top Party leaders and many parliamentary deputies. The Party was outlawed. In the nominally free Reichstag elections of March 5, it still received almost 5 million votes—which the government promptly declared invalid. The size of the vote could not disguise the fact that the Nazis had succeeded in smashing the Communist colossus into hundreds of dispersed leaderless groups and subgroups, that they had isolated the benumbed, confused, protesting, and resigned membership. Party headquarters were padlocked and sealed. The music of the Communist War Veterans was heard no more. The streets, now controlled by Nazis, rang with shouts of "Heil Hitler!"—an ugly, dangerous sound to Communist ears.

These dazed and helpless men found it hard to realize what had happened to them: After years of planning to "settle accounts with the enemy," they had been defeated. They became acquainted with the ice-cold breath of fear: in prison cells and the first concentration camps, in darkened rooms, attics, barns, and forests where they hid or met secretly. For the first time in their lives, some of these men now had to make important decisions on their own. For many of them, faith in the Party vanished; they had only one desire—not to be caught and tortured, not to have to sacrifice themselves for a hopeless cause. They wanted to live—even if it meant betrayal of the Party. This is how the Gestapo found stool pigeons and how the Nazi Party got new members.

Others tried to get out of politics altogether. Could you call a man a coward because he thought of his wife and children? Was it not true that Communists who tried to resist would end up in the hands of the Gestapo? Did this not prove that resistance was pointless? Those Communists who continued the fight refused to give in to such doubts. There were some who never doubted at all. Professional Party workers, had, of course, no choice. They were blacklisted; posters with their photographs appeared everywhere. They depended completely on the Party machine, and their only hope for survival lay in being sent out of the country. Besides, many Communists were sure that the whole nightmare would not last more than a few months—a year or two at most—and that their underground activities would help speed its end. Others were so conditioned by Party discipline that they unquestioningly obeyed whatever orders they received from the leaders that were left—even though the Party was now banned. Like good soldiers, they went on doing their work, distributing illegal leaflets and painting anti-Nazi slogans on walls and sidewalks under cover of night.

But neither dependence on the apparatus and the vain hope that Hitler's days were numbered, nor the habit of Party discipline quite explains the courageous resistance to Nazism of some German Communists. Many who died in the prisons and concentration camps of the Third Reich did so for their faith—just as Protestants, Catholics, and Jehovah's Witnesses did. When they took up the hopeless fight against the Nazi victors, they followed the dictates of their own conscience, they acted in accordance with their own principles. Many a Communist died without suspecting that his comrades had betrayed him. The traitors were not only those who had consciously sold out to the Nazis; no—thousands of Communists fell victim because of the insane policies of the Party apparatus.

The Communist high command had taken certain early precautions. In the summer of 1932, it had begun to prepare for underground operations because it had expected the von Papen government to outlaw the Party.* On January 30, 1933, the Party abandoned its headquarters in Karl Liebknecht Haus and began to go underground. And yet, despite these preparations, the leaders were thrown into complete confusion by the mass arrest following the Reichstag Fire. Thälmann's arrest on March 3, 1933, was the worst blow. Better security measures had to be devised to prevent further arrests of key members. Communication between the Party districts had to be restored. New officials had to be appointed to replace those arrested. And a successor for Thälmann had to be found.

Ulbricht, who escaped the wave of mass arrests, decided to try for the job. He could not, of course, hope to be elected to it as long as Thälmann was alive; at the moment it was simply a question of who was to take over responsibility in his absence.†

Ulbricht was not the only one who wanted this job. Two other members of the Party's Executive Committee, John Schehr and Hermann Schubert (who was Hamburg district secretary), had similar plans. An embittered power struggle began. Each of the three contenders tried by every means to increase his own influence, to find allies against the other

* Franz von Papen succeeded Brüning as Chancellor in June, 1932, but was repudiated by and expelled from the Catholic Center Party after acting independently of it in July when his *coup d'état* succeeded in bringing the downfall of the SPD Prime Minister of Prussia and other officials. Von Papen, whose cabinet represented the interests of the ultra-conservative *Junker* class, resigned in November, after two elections had failed to return a majority in the Reichstag.

† Thälmann died in 1944. He was murdered by the SS at Buchenwald in August of that year. He had never been officially put on trial.

two, and to place his own followers in key posts within the underground Party organization. Schehr could point to a Moscow directive giving him Thälmann's job. He had an important ally in Hans Kippenberger, who was head of the extremely important secret military arm of the KPD. Schubert could cite an earlier decision by the KPD's Politburo promising him the succession. He could also count on the fact that he was an intimate friend of Thälmann's and that he was in good standing with a number of the district secretaries. Only Ulbricht had nothing to show, and yet he proved to be the strongest in this war of succession.

So as not to have to fight on two fronts simultaneously, Ulbricht allied himself with Schubert while Schehr was away on a long trip to Moscow. It soon became clear that Schubert was no match for an experienced *apparatchik* like Ulbricht. Schubert decided to give up the struggle in the summer of 1933 and went to Prague, where he tried to rally a small group in his support. Later, he tried the same thing in the Saar. Schehr, on his part, had put too much trust in his Moscow directive and in his alliance with Kippenberger. He neglected his work with the district secretaries, whose reports were vitally important for his own reports to Moscow. This made available to Ulbricht an important source of information and powerful political support. He lost no time in exploiting his rival's weaknesses, and he also knew how to utilize his own strength.

"Ulbricht's strength," says Herbert Wehner in his memoirs, "lay in his tireless diligence. He showed it in all situations. He kept his co-workers and subordinates (he had to have subordinates) constantly busy and relentlessly supervised their work. His superiority to others did not stem from deeper insight or greater maturity, but from his ability always to be better informed than others and to be more persistent in the execution of details."

Ulbricht was nothing if not a conscientious conspirator. He knew that conspiracy has stringent rules and he applied them vigorously. Immediately after Thälmann's arrest, he demanded that all of "Teddy's drinking buddies" be ousted from the apparatus. This was a well-aimed thrust against Schehr and Schubert, who had been among Thälmann's hard-drinking friends, but undoubtedly it also sprang from Ulbricht's conviction that underground work was incompatible with any sort of dissipation, that it called for a strict, Spartan way of life. Ulbricht himself had no trouble living up to these abstemious principles.

It is not known where Ulbricht lived in the first months after Hitler came to power. But we know that in July, 1933, when Wilhelm Pieck left Germany, Ulbricht moved into his hideout in a Berlin suburb and stayed there until the beginning of October. His landlord said of him:

Ulbricht was extremely reserved. He simply stayed in his room most of the time and kept quiet. If you tried to talk to him, his forbidding frown soon discouraged you. At that time, we sometimes played ball in our garden, which was large and well hidden from the street. Our children and guests from the city enjoyed playing catch there. Now and then, Ulbricht joined us in one of these games. But even while playing, he spoke only in monosyllables and never fell into any kind of conversation with the people he played with. . . . Of course, we had no idea that this man living under our roof and eating my wife's cooking was the Reichstag Deputy Walter Ulbricht. Then, one day, we saw his picture in the paper as a man wanted by the police. The public was asked to be on the look-out for "enemies of the state" and, if possible, to hand them over to the police. Now we knew who our boarder was. I took some of the newspapers up to his room and suggested that it was high time for him to leave. He admitted that our house was getting too dangerous for him, but it took him several days to get ready to move out. Even then, he continued going out every evening after dark to take care of his "affairs."[1]

Ulbricht left Germany in early October to follow Pieck to Paris, where the German Communist leaders had established their headquarters. Since Communists were constantly being arrested within Germany, it had been decided to move the actual leadership to Paris and leave Schehr in charge of German underground operations. But Schehr was arrested by the Gestapo before the year was out; in February, 1934, he and two other functionaries were "shot while trying to escape."

This eliminated one of Ulbricht's rivals, but it did not put an end to the struggle over Thälmann's succession. Ulbricht, whose candidacy astonished those in the know—none of the potential leaders had thought him in the running—soon proved that even in exile he was easily the equal of, if not the superior to, any other top Party operator.

Exile in Paris and Popular Front Politics

The Communist Party leaders who lived in exile in Paris lived under assumed names, and only a very few carefully screened individuals knew their whereabouts. But whenever a Party functionary arrived from Germany to make a report, he was told—as soon as he had crossed the border—when and where to show up in Paris. Contact with the Party in Paris would usually be made at a café or some other spot; the visitor would find there some Paris-based Party member delegated to the job by one of the leaders. The Paris contact would tell him where to stay, would give him money, and would then let him know when and where he could finally meet one or more of the exiled leaders. Sometimes, couriers from Moscow reported to the publishing firm of Éditions du Carrefour on the Boulevard Montparnasse—the base of operations for the talented, well-known German Communist Willi Münzenberg, who had come to Paris in the spring of 1933 to start his anti-fascist, pro-Communist propaganda campaigns. Couriers reporting to the Éditions du Carrefour were usually sent on to the German Communist leaders in Paris; some of the money received by German Communists from Moscow also went through Münzenberg's clearinghouse.

When Ulbricht arrived in Paris, nobody there knew whether the Nazis planned to put Thälmann on trial. It was feared that Thälmann would be secretly convicted and secretly thrust into some remote provincial prison—a development that would definitely be against the exiled Party leaders' interests. What they wanted was a public trial, at which Thälmann would denounce the National Socialist state and thus bring worldwide publicity and glory to the German Communist Party. In this vain hope, they turned down all the offers made by Thälmann's lawyer, a Dr. Langbehn, to use his good connections with Nazi officials to get Thälmann off without a trial. Langbehn protested their inhumanity and dropped the case, but the exiled Communist leaders stuck to their guns. When, in the summer of 1934, some Berlin Communists made plans to liberate Thälmann, the leaders in Paris stopped them at the last minute. Thälmann the martyr was more valuable to them than Thälmann free. Besides, they were afraid the Gestapo might welcome such an attempt as a pretext to "shoot him while trying to escape."

There can be no doubt that Ulbricht profited by this policy and these decisions, for they clearly helped him in his fight to succeed Thälmann. Yet there is no proof that his position, shared by all the leaders in exile, was personally motivated. Humanitarian considerations have never, in any case, played a part in the world of Communist leadership. Politically speaking, the position of the exiled leaders in the Thälmann affair was in no way out of line with their established policy.

One of Ulbricht's jobs in exile was to write articles and pamphlets explaining the Party's policies after Hitler's rise to power. At first, his analyses of the political situation and the conclusions he drew differed little from those of other Party functionaries. Like the rest of them, he denied that the Party had been badly beaten and even spoke of a "new revolutionary upsurge":

> In the present period, with the revolutionary crisis coming to a head, with the victory of Socialism in the Soviet Union and the revolutionary upsurge in Germany . . . the order of the day demands that we . . . organize the fight for Soviet power. . . . But this is no short-range task. It means immediate formation of a revolutionary army with which to overthrow fascism by organizing all forms of resistance against fascism: from strikes, mass demonstrations, and political general strikes to armed revolt.

For Ulbricht, those who rejected this invitation to suicide were "opportunists":

> Opportunistic influences [can be detected] especially in the tendency to underestimate the proletariat's fighting power and to overestimate fascist strength, as in the statement, "The fascist dictatorship is no short-lived affair." Similarly, some people will tell you, "The German working class is incapable of defending the Soviet Union.". . . These tendencies to underestimate the revolutionary upsurge are closely tied up with the failure to link our immediate demands to general propaganda for Soviet power. To "forget". . . that Soviet power is our goal . . . is a typical sign of opportunism.[2]

Unfortunately, the quick attainment of this goal was blocked not only by the Nazis, but also—so the exiled Communist leaders insisted—by the Social Democrats. Ulbricht declared:

The Social Democratic policy of "waiting" and of discrediting Bolshevism plays into the hands of Hitler Fascism. We must unmask it now . . . so that, when the hour for battle arrives, the workers in every factory will easily be able to see how Social Democrats and Trotskyites are really serving Hitler Fascism. . . .[3] The kind of "democracy" the SPD demands is . . . a form of fascism, "authoritarian democracy" as practiced by Masaryk in Prague and Tardieu in Paris. . . . Under present conditions . . . "democracy" is a reactionary utopian fantasy. There is no road leading from fascism to democracy.[4]

German Social Democratic workers had to be "freed" as quickly as possible, then, "from the SPD," to "help them find the way to Communism" and to "win them as members of the KPD." In pursuit of this goal, almost any means were permissible. Only the most obvious method was taboo: to stop, look, and think. When some of the underground Communists in Germany dared to suggest that perhaps the KPD, too, might have made mistakes, Ulbricht enlightened them: "Developments have proved that the strategy and tactics of the KPD were absolutely correct."*

* The same argument was still being repeated almost three decades later by Ulbricht and his followers: "There is no break in the policy of the Party before and after the creation of the fascist dictatorship. On the contrary, there is a uniform and unbroken continuity in its major attack on the most reactionary forces of German imperialism and militarism." (Wolfgang Schumann, "Zur führenden Rolle unserer marxistisch-leninistischen Partei und ihres Zentral komitees im Kampf gegen Faschismus und Krieg, 1933–1945" ["The Leading Role of Our Marxist-Leninist Party and Its Central Committee in the Fight Against Fascism and War: 1933–1945"], *Zeitschrift für Geschichtswissenschaft* [an East Berlin history journal], No. 5, 1962.)

Soon, however—indeed, almost simultaneously with the appearance of these statements—the Kremlin began to devise a new strategy that was to knock the earlier policies of the exiled German Communists into a cocked hat. For the Comintern leaders were impressed by the way French Communists, Socialists, and left-wing bourgeois Radical Socialists jointly opposed the fascist demonstrations in Paris of early February, 1934, that had led to the downfall of the Daladier government. The Comintern decided, therefore, to shift its troops from the extreme left, as it were, to the center of the international scene. From this new position, it would fight fascism shoulder to shoulder with its new allies: the Socialists, the progressive bourgeoisie, etc. In other words: The democrats were no longer the enemy; they were allies in the fight against fascism.

But to win the Social Democrats and other anti-fascists over to a united front was no easy matter, considering that the Communists had called them "Social Fascists" and worse for many years. First, the Communists would have to don new uniforms, rip the Soviet star from their caps, and hide the old emblems in their back pockets. The old battlecry "For Soviet Power!" was not going to win over the democratic elements. The new motto had to be, "For the Popular Front Against Fascism!"

With the Comintern pushing hard for a Popular Front, Communist officers and troops who wanted to know what the new task was had only to read Walter Ulbricht's article quoted above. It was a perfect compendium of everything that was now completely unacceptable: an unrealistic appraisal of the situation; a violent attack on Social Democrats; stubborn adherence to now outmoded strategy and tactics; an open rejection of democracy.

The new turn in Comintern policy affected various German

Communist leaders in different ways. And, of course, it set off new factional struggles that continued until the Great Purge in the Soviet Union put a terrible end to them.[5]

Everyone knew that Georgi Dimitrov, the leader of the Bulgarian Communist Party, head of the Comintern's Balkan section, and hero of the Reichstag Fire trial, had played a key role in shaping the new strategy, but opinions differed as to exactly how much influence he had in Moscow. Ulbricht and Pieck, for their part, banked on the Bulgarian and on the new policy of the Popular Front. Had they realized, then, that their earlier policies bordered on madness? Most of the exiled German Communist leaders—Wilhelm Florin, Franz Dahlem, Hermann Schubert, Fritz Heckert, and Fritz Schulte—thought that Moscow was only playing along with Dimitrov because of his momentary international popularity. They considered Dimitrov a "conciliator" and felt it was safer to keep away from him.

Dimitrov was, however, hard at work. His preparations for the Seventh World Congress of the Comintern included a detailed discussion of the merits of the united-front policy:

You will see from the enclosed rough draft what approach I take in my report on the second point of the agenda. In addition, I . . . would like to raise the following questions:

I. *On Social Democracy.* (1) Is it correct to describe Social Democracy as Social Fascism? By this attitude, we often bar our own way to Social Democratic workers. (2) Is it correct always and everywhere to label Social Democracy as the chief prop of the bourgeoisie? . . . (4) Is it correct to deal with the leading members of the Social Democratic Parties and the reformist trade unions, collectively and individually, as conscious traitors to the working class? Finally, isn't it to be expected that in the course of the joint struggle with Social Democratic workers, responsible leaders of the Social Democratic Parties and reformist unions will come over to the revolutionary road? Is it not in our interest to make this transition easier in every possible way and so to accelerate the movement of the Social Democratic workers to our side? . . .

II. *On the United Front.* . . . (2) We must abandon the view that only a "united front from below" can be created and that every corresponding appeal to the Social Democratic Party leadership is opportunism. (3) The fighting initiative of the masses must be developed without petty domination of the united front organizations by the Communist Parties; no *declamations* on the hegemony of the Communist Party, but realization of its leadership through *practical work.*[6]

By October, 1934, Comintern leaders were clearly favoring the Pieck-Ulbricht minority within the KPD. The majority of the German Communist leaders nevertheless tried to continue in their opposition to the Popular Front. They assumed, with some reason, that Stalin had not yet decided definitely in favor of it. At a conference of KPD leaders in Moscow called by the Comintern in January, 1935, the two sides fought the issue out with a vehemence that almost led to blows. Though in the majority, opponents of the Popular Front strategy continued to lose ground. The resolution of the Central Committee issued at the close of the meeting revealed what line the conference had taken:

The Central Committee, in self-critical fashion, has recognized that these errors, shortcomings, and weaknesses of our party work must be blamed primarily on a sectarian approach in all spheres of mass work, especially with regard to the policy of the united front and to opportunistic speculations that fascism would wreck itself and that a spontaneous mass movement would develop. Fascism does not collapse automatically. . . . The overthrow of the Hitler dictatorship is the central task of the proletariat and must be accompanied by winning over allies from all strata of the working masses, by creating the broadest anti-fascist Popular Front as the basis for a people's revolution whose goal is a free Socialist Germany resting on council power![7]

Gradually it became clear to all the factions involved that the forthcoming Seventh World Congress of the Communist International would put an end to all this intra-party struggle. Then and there Stalin would show which faction he favored. Both sides worked feverishly in the months preceding the Congress—after several postponements it had been scheduled for July, 1935, in Moscow—to influence the coming decision.

At this point, Ulbricht suddenly tried for a *rapprochement* with the left wing of the Social Democratic leadership, then located in Prague, and his articles and essays were now designed—albeit somewhat ineptly—to help bring this about.* The fact that he had enough initiative to make this switch and write the pieces at all completely confused the anti-Ulbricht faction. Whenever they could, they tried in their turn to stress the point that *they*, the majority faction, were Thälmann's true heirs, that Pieck and Ulbricht were trying to "liquidate

---

* To be sure, while Ulbricht urged "unity of action for the sake of the immediate interests of the struggle against Hitler Fascism," he simultaneously attacked the SPD Executive Committee and said that those Social Democratic members and groups who had "seen through" the policies of the SPD leadership must become "members of the Communist Party"; like Marx and Engels, they should call themselves Communists, since the "creation of working-class unity can only be attained through united action and by winning the working masses for the revolutionary class struggle, for the struggle to achieve Communism. . . . We shall . . . do everything to win the working masses to Communist principles and to membership in the KPD, to that policy that has led to the victory of Socialism in the Soviet Union." ("Für die Aktionseinheit gegen den Hitler-Faschismus—Offene Antwort an Siegfried Aufhäuser und die linken Sozialdemokraten" ["For United Action Against Hitler-Fascism: An Open Reply to Siegfried Aufhäuser and the Left Social Democrats"], *Rundschau,* No. 55, 1934.)

his heritage." In addition, they attempted to prove that Thälmann had wanted a united KPD-SPD front all along but that
the profoundly reactionary nature of the Social Democratic
Party had frustrated his efforts to create one. Hurriedly,
Florin, Schulte, and Schubert sent an emissary to Berlin to
find witnesses to vouch for the truth of their argument. Meanwhile, Ulbricht collected material in Paris.

Couriers who came to the Paris Party headquarters to report on underground operations in Germany usually tended
to exaggerate the success of their work. This was quite customary; everyone knew they exaggerated, everyone accepted
the fact that they *had* to—if for no other reason than to get
money from Moscow. But Walter Ulbricht set out to discover,
from a few trusted friends, what was what in the German
Party. Next, he prevailed upon the couriers to tell him "the
real truth" after they had made their official reports to the
Party leaders. And when those leaders went to Moscow to
report on KPD affairs, Ulbricht waited until they had finished
with their usual "window dressing"—their exaggerated reports on operations in Germany—and then presented his own
information. It not only came much closer to the truth, but
also made out a far better case for the proposed new Popular
Front policy than the trumped-up success stories. In addition,
he was thus able to show up the exiled Party leaders as dishonest braggarts:

> The reports of comrades from Germany were objective as ever.
> . . . Ulbricht noted down everything they said—about strikes
> against Hitler's "workers' front," about sabotage, secret or-
> ganizations, and the growing discontent of the workers.
>   Finally Ulbricht took the young men away with him, on
> some friendly pretext. . . . He took them to a nearby café
> where he went over the whole proceedings again and, after
> uttering brief threats, got them to give him a true and au-

thentic report on conditions in Germany. They admitted that
Hitler's workers' front was as solid as a rock, that the strike
action attempted by small trade-union groups was pointless
and ineffective, and that the Nazis, far from immediately arresting malcontents, knew how to win them over. . . . Once
again Ulbricht wrote everything down, and then he praised
the messengers, saying that a true Bolshevik must always
honor the truth. . . .

For years he collected "authentic material" in this fashion.
He never warned his chairman or suggested to him that he
was over-optimistic. He fattened his victim, whose death would
bring him his reward. . . . When he considered that the moment had come, he struck. His *dossier* was devastating. His
rival was exposed as a painter of over-hopeful pictures, which,
to the order then prevailing in the Kremlin, was synonymous
with counterrevolution—and with death.[8]

To the surprise of friend and foe alike, Ulbricht's diligent
efforts on behalf of the "new line" at first remained unre-
warded. Although the Seventh World Congress demonstrated
that Moscow had decided in favor of the Popular Front policy,
Ulbricht received neither public acclaim nor promotion.*

* In the wake of the de-Stalinization process, Ulbricht described the
achievement of the Popular Front in this way:
"We, too, the members and leaders of the KPD, suffered under Stalin's
cult of personality and his terrorist methods. . . . Our Politburo fought
Stalinist methods and received understanding and support from Soviet
comrades and the General Secretary of the Communist International,
Comrade Georgi Dimitrov. Our Politburo developed the Popular Front
policy and the national policy of uniting all forces against Hitler, together with Soviet comrades and such outstanding leaders of the international workers' movement as Maurice Thorez, Palmiro Togliatti,
Klement Gottwald, and Harry Pollitt. We had to do it against the resistance of some of the leading functionaries in our own Party. Comrade
Wilhelm Pieck and I succeeded in winning a majority of the Party's
Central Committee to this policy. . . . [But] Comrade Georgi Dimitrov's
proposals were chiefly responsible for the turn in policy. . . . Without
. . . Comrade Dimitrov's support, it would have been harder for our

He was elected candidate (nonvoting) member of the Executive Committee of the Comintern (ECCI), but he had held this position since 1928. On the other hand, Wilhelm Florin, one of Ulbricht's adversaries, not only became a member but was elected Secretary of the Executive Committee.

Immediately after the Seventh World Congress, the German Communist Party held its own "Brussels"* conference in the town of Ruhlevo, near Moscow, in October, 1935. Here, Ulbricht did chalk up one great success: After long and violent debates and much recrimination between the factions, the delegates decided not to re-elect Schubert and Schulte, two of the most determined opponents of the Popular Front policy, to the Central Committee.† This removed yet another of Ulbricht's rivals, Schulte, from the scene of battle. From now on, Ulbricht was a figure to be reckoned with among the German leaders in Paris. Though Pieck's prestige within the

---

Party leadership to lessen the effects of the Stalin cult of personality on our Party and to execute the policy that corresponded to the Seventh World Congress decisions." (Speech to the SED Central Committee, *Neues Deutschland*, April 14, 1963.)

* This designation was used to mislead the Gestapo.

† In the meantime, several supporters of the "Majority" had gone over to the "Minority." Manuilsky and Togliatti, who attended the meeting as representatives of the Comintern, prevailed upon Pieck to announce—before the new Central Committee was elected—"that they, in the interest of preserving the continuity of the Party's policy and to demonstrate the link between the young cadres and the tradition-rich old cadres, considered it correct and useful to re-elect Schubert and Schulte to the Central Committee. Likewise, they voiced their fear that if the two were not re-elected, the fierce debates might be interpreted as a break with the Party's past." (Herbert Wehner, *Erinnerungen*, pp. 105 ff.) Wehner was one of those who spoke firmly against the proposal, and, after his speech, the conference voted against it.

Thälmann, Pieck, Florin, Heckert, Ulbricht, Dahlem, Merker, Wehner, Ackermann—as members of or candidates for the Politburo—and Bertz, Weber, Irene Gärtner (i.e., Elli Schmidt), Hähnel, Münzenberg, Mewis, and Knöchel were elected to the new Central Committee.

KPD was greater, he could not hold a candle to Ulbricht when it came to manipulating the Party machine.

From Moscow, Ulbricht returned to Western Europe, and, in accordance with the Seventh World Congress decisions, he tried to establish contact with *émigré* leaders of the SPD. On November 10, 1935, he wrote to the Executive Committee of the SPD proposing that the leaders of both parties jointly appeal to all Social Democrats and Communists in Germany to "act together in a spirit of comradeship." On November 23, Ulbricht and Dahlem—who had by then switched to Ulbricht's winning faction*—went to Prague to talk to the Social Democrats in person. The representatives of the SPD Executive Committee, Hans Vogel and Friedrich Stampfer, informed them, however, that Ulbricht's proposal had been rejected; the KPD had not yet proved its sincerity.

Ulbricht himself had given the Social Democrats cause to be suspicious: In his speech at the World Congress on the aims of a German Popular Front, he had said, "In the struggle for Soviet power, it is possible—during a political crisis—to establish an anti-fascist Popular Front, so long as the masses are still not ready for a Soviet government. Later on, when conditions have improved, we can continue the struggle for a proletarian dictatorship. . . . The goal of our fight is a Soviet Germany."[9]

---

* SED leaders give different versions of Dahlem's position during the disputes on the Popular Front policy. After Dahlem had fallen into disgrace in 1953, Wilhelm Pieck put it this way: "[Walter Ulbricht] waged a tenacious and consistent struggle against the false estimate of the situation and against the sectarianism of the group of Central Committee members whose spokesmen were Schubert, Schulte and Dahlem." (*Einheit*, No. 7, 1953.) But after Dahlem's rehabilitation, Alexander Abusch wrote that "Comrade Ulbricht defended the new policy with utmost consistency; Comrades Wilhelm Pieck and Fritz Heckert were the first to stand at his side, Comrade Franz Dahlem supported him in the foreign-affairs secretariat of the Party." (*Einheit*, No. 6, 1963.)

Angry and disappointed by his failure in Prague, Ulbricht yielded to the temptation of replying publicly to the SPD's rebuff early in 1936. The "brutal rejection of a United Front," he wrote, came about because not enough pressure had been exerted from "below" on the SPD leaders who, by their "class collaboration policy," bore "historic responsibility for the victory of fascism." As if intent on proving to the Social Democrats how right they had been to distrust him, he added, "We Communists fight for democratic freedom because it gives greater mobility to the working class and its organizations, and permits them to prepare the masses for the battle for Soviet power."[10]

The Communist leaders had better luck in Paris than in Prague. As early as the winter of 1935, a number of anti-Hitler refugees had been willing to join the Communists in a Popular Front. With Nazi power solidly entrenching itself in Germany, these anti-fascists were carried away by the Seventh World Congress and by the Communists' continued assurances of sincerity.

The founders of the Popular Front met at the Hotel Lutetia (later to become the Gestapo's headquarters in Paris) in 1936 and established a provisional committee. Its members were a varied group: prominent, although nonpolitical, members of the middle class; representatives of the Socialist Workers Party (SAP*); members of the KPD. The Social Democrats Rudolf Breitscheid and Max Braun joined the committee as individuals, since their Executive Committee had not authorized them to represent the SPD in the Popular Front.

At the beginning, the Communist representatives on the

* An SPD splinter group, which also included Communists who had been expelled from the KPD in 1928 as "right-wing deviationists" and "conciliators."

Popular Front Committee were Herbert Wehner, Paul Merker, and Willi Münzenberg, who had played an important part in setting up the Paris section of the Popular Front.[11] Non-Communist members were Professors Bernhard, Denicke, and Gumbel, Jakob Walcher—of the Socialist Workers Party, Fritz Sternberg, and Rudolf Breitscheid. The novelist Heinrich Mann served as president of the Committee; Max Braun was chairman. But after a few months, the Communist members changed, and Ulbricht and Merker alone took on the job. It took them only a few weeks to come into open conflict with the non-Communists. In June, 1937, and again at a meeting in September, they were openly accused of sabotaging decisions made by the Committee, and their colleagues demanded that they abandon their divisive tactics and help to re-establish the former "basis of trust and comradeship." Ulbricht and Merker promised, but there was no change.

At another meeting in September, Heinrich Mann spoke out against "lack of trust and solidarity caused by various disloyal acts on the part of the Communist representatives." Professor Bernhard charged that the Communists had "misled" the Committee; Braun accused them of repeated "attempts at deception." The indignant Committee members decided to submit their complaints in a letter to the KPD Central Committee and to ask the Communist leadership to put an end to the "untenable situation brought on by the behavior of the Communist representatives in the Popular Front Committee."

Heinrich Mann and his group were thoroughly confounded when their complaint was answered in writing by Ulbricht himself, who said that his letter constituted the Central Committee's official reply. They wrote again to the Central Committee, and this second letter, answered by a half-hearted apology over Pieck's signature, sheds interesting light on

Ulbricht's activities. In it, the majority of the Committee members accused him of lying and of distorting facts, and said that he as well as Merker had been engaged in the attempt to "set up a Popular Front that was to be run exclusively by the Communist Party":

> Walter Ulbricht tries to blame the non-Communist members for every new problem that arises. But his most outrageous lie, in a letter crawling with falsehoods, is his accusation that [the non-Communists] are being manipulated by "dark powers behind the scenes". . . . and that they are planning a united front with "big capitalists, right-wing Catholic leaders, and Reichswehr generals."
>
> This is not only an affront to all non-Communist members of the Popular Front Committee; it is sheer nonsense. . . . The truth is [that] the Communist representatives, especially Ulbricht, were the ones who blocked every attempt at socialization and expropriation, because they wanted to keep a door open for the big capitalist circles. . . . May we remind Ulbricht that last year he himself suggested in all seriousness that Otto Strasser* and his followers be invited to join the Popular Front? Breitscheid and his Social Democratic friends prevented this, which is probably the reason why Ulbricht now accuses them of being Strasser's allies.

And Heinrich Mann's anger with Ulbricht shows clearly in a letter he wrote to Max Braun on October 25, 1937:

> Your report of October 23 makes it evident that Ulbricht is indeed trying to start his own Popular Front with himself in command. Much as I dislike regarding members of the German Opposition as my enemies, there are some who evidently

---

* Otto Strasser was a Nazi from 1925 to 1930. He then broke with Hitler and founded the Fighting Union of Revolutionary National Socialists (Black Front). He had left Germany in 1933.

want just that. This is why I oppose calling a plenary committee meeting, as long as U. is allowed to appear there as
chief representative of his Party, or even as a representative.[12]

"You see," Mann added, in a letter to Alfred Kantorowicz,
"I simply can't sit down at the same table with a man who
suddenly claims that the table at which we are sitting is not
a table at all but a duck pond and expects me to agree with
him."[13]

Münzenberg forwarded these and other complaints to Moscow. As a result, Dahlem replaced Ulbricht in the Paris section of the KPD in the spring of 1938, and later, Ulbricht
was put on trial by the Comintern's Control Commission. But
the Popular Front Committee never recovered from the grave
crisis of late 1937. One non-Communist member after another
was forced to conclude that it was impossible to work with
the Communists on an equal basis, and the Committee became a dead letter. "If difficulties arose in the Provisional
Popular Front Committee in Paris," wrote Ulbricht, "their
causes were deeply rooted in the shortcomings of the United
Front. The KPD participated in the Popular Front Committee as an organization, while the Social Democratic comrades
acted only as individuals without organizational support; unfortunately, they had not yet attained an adequate understanding of the country's problems. . . . No one can really
fight fascism so long as he does not contribute to the strength-
ening of the most important bulwark in this struggle, the
Soviet Union."[14]

Yet it would be wrong to say that Ulbricht personally
destroyed the Popular Front. For, after all, during that particular phase of Communist policy, he acted—as always—on
strict orders from Moscow. And it appears that by the end of

1937, the Kremlin had lost interest in the Popular Front idea.*

But even had this not been the case, the Popular Front was, sooner or later, destined to collapse. Every time the Communists chalked up any kind of success with their new "unity" approach, they quickly remembered Lenin's dictum that the Communist Party must always lead, never follow, which made it impossible for them to recognize any ally as an equal. In other words, alliance with other groups always ended in hostility, on the grounds that any ally who will not knuckle under must be treated as an enemy. This was why the French Communists at first supported and then denounced but in any case refused to participate in Léon Blum's Popular Front government of 1936: They would rather criticize it and put pressure on it from the outside. And for the same reason, the Comintern, during the Spanish Civil War, ordered the liquidation of thousands of Catalan Anarchists and Socialists who refused to take orders from the Communists.†

* An article by Dimitrov published in *L'Humanité*, the French Communist newspaper, on November 12, 1937, corroborates this theory. It says, "Comrade Stalin was a thousand times right when he wrote ten years ago that capitalism cannot be defeated before Social Democracy is liquidated in the workers' movement." This was, to all practical purposes, a repudiation of the Popular Front. (See Babette L. Gross, "Die Volksfrontpolitik in den dreissiger Jahren" ("The Popular Front Policy in the 1930's"), supplement to *Das Parlament*, October 24, 1962.)

† Opinions differ as to just what part Ulbricht played in the Spanish Civil War. Pieck's statement that Ulbricht fought in the International Brigades (*Einheit*, No. 7, 1953, on the occasion of Ulbricht's sixtieth birthday) is obviously false; even Becher, in his official Ulbricht biography, does not go beyond saying that Ulbricht addressed "the working men of Germany" via Radio Barcelona in 1937. Alfred Kantorowicz, who was in Spain himself, reports that Ulbricht spent only a few weeks "in Barcelona, Valencia, and possibly Albacete" in December, 1936, "to check up on the political machines of the International Brigades" (*Die Welt*, March 2, 1963). This corresponds with Wehner's opinion that

The attitude of the French Communists and the horrors in Spain gave non-Communist supporters of the Popular Front all over the world food for thought. German Socialist *émigrés* and democrats noted—not without profound shock—the striking parallel between the French and Spanish events and Ulbricht's and Merker's behavior in the Popular Front. While pursuing a Leninist policy of alliance, Communists throughout the world were also supporting Stalin's foreign policy. They not only fought fascism under the Popular Front; they also fought for Moscow's interests with all the strength and cunning at their command. They made common cause with non-Communist allies against a common enemy, but as for planning or working toward a common goal, that was out of the question. Even in the period of greatest concessions to their temporary allies, the Communists never lost sight of the idea that bourgeois democracy was only a starting point for the attainment of Soviet power.

As early as 1931, Stalin said to Heinz Neumann, a German Communist, "Don't you agree that if the National Socialists should come to power in Germany, they would concentrate so completely on the West that we would be left to build Socialism in peace?"[15] Stalin held fast to the idea of

"Ulbricht spent only a few, brief periods in Spain. . . . But as a Politburo leader, Ulbricht had connections with the 'cadres' . . . namely, those who supervised the German Communists fighting in Spain" (from a letter to the author, March 20, 1964). Erich Wollenberg writes that the German Socialist Kurt Landau was arrested by German members of the Barcelona apparatus and tortured to death in a GPU (Russian secret police) prison in Spain—by order of Walter Ulbricht and the French Communist André Marty, who commanded the International Brigades. ("Der Apparat: Stalins Fünfte Kolonne" ["The *Apparat:* Stalin's Fifth Column"], [*Ostprobleme*, No. 19, 1951].) In the 1950's, Marty supposedly confessed to a girl friend that he had given in to Ulbricht's demand that Landau be liquidated (from a letter from Wollenberg to the author, October 2, 1963). My research has borne out the data furnished by Kantorowicz and Wehner.

his being the victorious third party while fascists and democrats fought it out. Working behind the scenes of the Popular
Front drama, he hoped fascism and democracy would weaken
each other. It was this attitude that enabled him to form an
alliance with the democracies against fascism, and then to
turn about—in the German-Soviet Nonaggression Pact—and
become an ally of fascism against the democracies.

Yet the macabre aspects of Communist Popular Front
policy should have been apparent years before the Stalin-
Hitler Pact. Had not the savage Soviet purge been carried
out during the Popular Front period? If so many decent anti-
Nazis had not been completely blinded by their justified fear
and hatred of National Socialism, they would have had to see
from reading the indictments of the Moscow trials that the
Popular Front was doomed when Stalin made political considerations the key factor in deciding who was a fascist, when
he equated internal opposition with fascism. The Popular
Front became a kind of bitter joke, when tens of thousands of
innocent people as well as Stalin's personal rivals were
branded as "fascist agents."

The Great Purge in the Soviet Union

Ulbricht, like so many other frightened but loyal functionaries, endorsed the Moscow trials and drew the proper political conclusions:

> Counterrevolutionary Trotskyism, in alliance with German
> Fascism, is the chief warmonger in the world; it is also the
> mortal enemy of the Soviet Union and of the international
> proletariat. The German Communist Party has a special ob-
> ligation to enlighten the Party, the Social Democratic masses,
> and all peace-loving people in Germany about the dangers of
> Trotskyism. It is the enemy of the people. It is particularly

dangerous to the anti-fascist movement in Germany because it works hand in glove with the Gestapo.[16]

In 1939, Ulbricht still insisted that "Trotskyite spies of Nazi Fascism" were "betraying brave anti-fascists to the Gestapo."[17] Did he really believe this? When Communist leaders discussed the question, Ulbricht always maintained that everything was "perfectly clear and simple." Wehner reports that Ulbricht considered the Soviet purge a "brilliant example of how the Socialist State ruthlessly eradicates its 'fifth column' before it can do any harm." The purges gave German Communist leaders the welcome pretext to accuse dissident Party members of being "Trotskyite spies" and to make them tractable through the threat inherent in this charge, or if that did not work, to render them "harmless."

Most of the German Communists who had managed to emigrate were financially dependent on the Party. They knew all too well what it would mean to become *persona non grata* with the Party leaders: no more money, ostracism by their comrades, trouble with foreign government authorities, sometimes even expulsion from the country. Communists willing to risk all these dangers ran the even graver risk of being given a Communist "state funeral": The leaders-in-exile might decide to send a dissident back to Germany to "prove himself in underground work" there. Amateurishly faked passports, perhaps intentionally bungled, or unsafe border crossings were a simple expedient for handing the returning comrade over to the Gestapo. Sometimes a Communist returning to Germany would be directed to an ex-Party-member turned stool-pigeon; and thus a genuine traitor unwittingly would continue to serve his former Party masters. The condemned man ran—unsuspectingly, or with only a premonition of what awaited him—into the baited trap.

What about those who had stayed in Germany to do underground work, and who perhaps had become self-confident with their small successes in anti-Nazi activities? Some of them had belonged to one of the opposition factions before 1933. They, too, were endangered by the Party apparatus. Ulbricht and other expatriate leaders decided that their comrades in Germany had to be warned against "Trotskyites" and other "Gestapo agents." Over the objections of a few Party officers, they sent out "warning lists" and circulars of the names and addresses of these unfortunates, complete with descriptions of their political activities and their "crimes" (usually "Trotskyism").* Sooner or later, these lists reached not only the illegal workers but the Gestapo as well. Any dissident Communist who managed to escape arrest for a time was inviting his doom. Was not his almost miraculous good luck proof that he had an "in" with the Gestapo?[18]

For almost ten years, German Communists lived in the shadow of death and danger. Whether in Germany or in exile, they were surrounded by intrigue, suspicion, betrayal. And if they went to the country on which all their hopes were centered, the country they regarded as a sanctuary, the country they cherished and loved—they were thrown in prisons and death camps, tortured, starved to death in the wastes of Kazakhstan, or delivered back to their worst enemy, the Gestapo.

No sooner had the Soviet purge begun, than agents from Moscow arrived in Paris to collect data on the German Com-

---

* "The 'warning lists' were really a continuation of the 'black lists' that the Kippenberger *apparat* had issued and distributed for years. Although after the Brussels Conference in 1935, it was decided to create a new organizational basis for all defense and security work against the Gestapo, both Hermann Nuding and Paul Bertz obviously continued to carry on these activities." (Wehner, letter to the author, March 20, 1964.)

munists there.* The German Communists in France had some
idea of what was happening in Russia, but tried to close their
eyes to it. Many fled to the International Brigades in Spain.
But those who were ordered to Moscow had to face up to the
terrible truth.

Foreign Communists, including German functionaries who
had earlier fled to the Soviet Union with their families, lived
in Moscow in the Hotel Lux, whose fading splendor dated
back to Czarist days. Here, the secret police (NKVD) appeared every night, searched the rooms, and marched off with
their latest victims, leaving terror and despair in their wake.
The women—wives, daughters, sisters—provided they themselves had not been arrested, would rush from prison to
prison, trying to find out where their husbands, fathers, or
brothers had been taken. If a colleague failed to show up at
work, one assumed he had been arrested during the night,
and one would try to be calm and unconcerned, as if it were
no surprise; but all who had had any personal contact with
the missing man feared they might be next on the list. The
Communists began to shun each other. To confide in anyone
was a dangerous luxury. They were fearful and suspicious of
any stranger who asked questions, no matter how harmless.
He could, after all, be a spy setting a trap. They lay awake
at night waiting for those ominous footsteps; by day, cor-
roded with fear, they kowtowed to the "great Stalin," demanded loudly that "the enemies of the people" be eradi-
cated, and betrayed their friends.

German Communists in Moscow disappeared one by one
into the NKVD cellars and the slave-labor camps. Only very

* For example, the German Communist Party functionary Grete Wilde,
who was active in the Comintern, came to Paris to collect information on
people working in the Münzenberg apparatus. (Wehner, *op. cit.*)

few had not been "deviationists" at some time during factional Party fights; now this "deviationism" served as the pretext for arrest. Among the first to be arrested in the purge were men like Schubert and Schulte who had opposed the Popular Front strategy out of loyalty to Thälmann. Now they were accused of having handed Thälmann over to the Gestapo. Indeed, Ulbricht himself remarked in 1939 that "the Trotskyite traitors betrayed Ernst Thälmann to the Gestapo. This must serve as a permanent warning to all honorable freedom fighters in Germany ruthlessly to purge the Trotskyite spies from the ranks of the working class and the anti-fascist movement."[19]

It became more and more difficult to see sense in the arrests. Terror raged blindly and unchecked. Many never discovered the nature of their alleged crimes. Others were confronted with fellow prisoners who implicated them in their "confessions." In all, only a few German Communists in Russia were spared. Even Ulbricht must have trembled for his freedom when he was called before the Comintern Central Committee in 1937. But he took great pains to discover exactly what it was that the Comintern wanted to hear before he wrote his report. He was careful not to make any false move. "I asked Ulbricht about the main line of his report," Wehner reports. "He replied that he was still working on it, but I couldn't believe he was stupid enough to commit himself in writing before he learned from Dimitrov, Manuilsky, Ercoli [Togliatti], and Kuusinen what questions they were going to raise." Ulbricht's care was rewarded: He was allowed to go back to Paris. But in 1938, Ulbricht returned to Moscow, where, after his case was closed, he became the KPD's permanent representative to the Comintern.

Historians and journalists have attempted to trace the fate

of German Communists in Hitler's Germany and the Soviet Union. The record speaks for itself:

The SS and Gestapo murdered two KPD Politburo members, Ernst Thälmann and John Schehr.

Four Politburo members were liquidated in the great Soviet purge—Hermann Remmele, Heinz Neumann, Fritz Schulte, and Hermann Schubert.

Nine members of the KPD Central Committee died or were murdered in German prisons and concentration camps.

Ten members of the KPD Central Committee were murdered in the Soviet Union. Among the best-known victims of the NKVD were: Hugo Eberlein, the German delegate to the First Congress of the Comintern, who had also been one of the founders of the KPD; Hans Kippenberger, head of the KPD's military apparatus; Leo Flieg, the Party's Organizational Secretary; Willy Leow, head of the Roten Frontkämpferbund (League of Communist War Veterans); Willi Koska, head of Roten Hilfe (Red Relief); Heinrich Süsskind and Werner Hirsch, editors-in-chief, and editors Erich Birkenhauer, Alfred Rebe, Theodor Beutling and Heinrich Kurella (brother of Alfred Kurella, now a well-known functionary of the East German Communist Party) of the newspaper *Rote Fahne*; Kurt Sauerland, the Party's theoretician; and Felix Halle, the lawyer for the Central Committee.

It is still not known how many other less prominent German Communists died in Russian prisons and slave-labor camps, or how many were forced—even before the German-Russian Nonaggression Pact—to leave Russia and return to Germany.* It has often been said, particularly in the Federal Republic, that Ulbricht was responsible for the ghastly fate

---

* In the following passages, I am indebted to the account given by Wehner.

of many of them,* but this accusation is not just. Ulbricht was not even in Moscow during the purge, but in Paris, although he went to Moscow occasionally for conferences. Besides, the NKVD did not ask expatriate German Party leaders who should or should not be arrested. At first, the victims were selected from files kept by the Comintern or the NKVD itself, files that often predated the purge. True, the "lists of offenses" contained in them were usually the outgrowth of mutual accusations by opposing Party factions. But how were those who made these accusations and denunciations to know the catastrophic effect they were to have?

No doubt, these "personnel files" contained denunciations by Ulbricht and by his enemies; no doubt, Ulbricht continued to deliver incriminating material against his foes even after the purge started—and, no doubt, his jailed enemies retaliated during their interrogations. But there was one major difference: The accusations against Ulbricht were not acted upon, whereas Ulbricht's charges were often tantamount to a death sentence. Those who accuse Ulbricht of having persecuted his comrades in the Soviet Union are really criticizing him for something else—for having survived.

True, other foreign Party leaders, Dimitrov among them, tried harder and more successfully than did Pieck and Ulbricht to help those arrested. But it cannot be said that the two Germans did nothing at all. Constantly beleaguered by wives of arrested men imploring them to do something for their innocent husbands, and by Communists ordered back to Germany desperately begging for intervention on their

---

* This is the claim of a pamphlet published in the Federal Republic by the "SED Opposition" under the title *Die Ulbricht-Legende* (*The Ulbricht Legend*): "From 1936 to 1939, Ulbricht coldbloodedly handed over to the GPU naïve comrades who had sought shelter in the U.S.S.R. from the fascist hangmen, and he approved their being put to death."

behalf, Ulbricht acted in a few cases, but he reported after-ward that the NKVD had been "utterly unapproachable."

Several German Communists who were released from prison had the courage to tell Pieck, Florin, and Ulbricht how they and their fellow prisoners had been treated. Some, they reported, had been released only because they had agreed to work as spies for the NKVD. One young man, for instance, told Florin and Pieck he had been assigned to spy on them—a piece of information that, understandably, upset the two leaders. Yet nonetheless, the three Germans did intervene on behalf of some prisoners, although without much success.

Wehner reports:

> After having been repeatedly petitioned by Pieck, Manuilsky said that he simply could not understand why Pieck was tak-ing up the cause of the arrested men. After all, most of them had confessed to working for the Gestapo or other hostile forces. Since no one could or would suggest that these con-fessions were obtained by force, it was obvious that those who had signed them were, to say the least, unreliable. What good could such men be to the Party? How would such people behave in the hands of the Gestapo, under torture? Manuilsky asked.

Since Stalin's death, many German victims of the purge have been posthumously "rehabilitated." Yet Ulbricht has not been able to bring himself to make public the rehabilita-tion of even one. On the contrary: SED leaders are said to have informed the families of rehabilitated purge victims that no public statement would be permitted.

The German-Soviet Nonaggression Pact

Those German Communists who survived the purge were soon to find that the price they had to pay was high indeed:

On August 23, 1939, Stalin and Hitler signed the German-Soviet Nonaggression Pact. The Pact included a secret protocol on sharing the expected spoils of war in Eastern Europe, the division of Poland, and the annexation of the Baltic states. Stalin's alliance with their worst enemy was an unimaginable humiliation for German Communists and plunged many of them into utter confusion and despair. In January, 1940, the surviving German Communist leaders came to Moscow for a conference with top Comintern functionaries to discuss the line the KPD was to take.*

Dimitrov began by declaring that the German Communist Party had not been an active political force since the Spanish Civil War, that it practically no longer existed. But, he said, the Pact with Hitler's Germany opened up new opportunities and new possibilities for Communist activity in Germany. Reports on the situation in Germany, German newspaper articles, and the widespread interest in the Soviet Pavilion at the 1939 Leipzig Trade Fair all pointed to the fact that the German people were becoming tremendously interested in the Soviet Union. Besides, Nazi supporters were showing strong signs of "differentiation." The war was bound to produce sudden revolutionary developments. It was imperative that various political centers be established, especially in Germany. These centers would later be combined in a unified organization to be called the Socialist Unity Party.

Four years later, when this Moscow conference was discussed at the treason trial of Wilhelm Knöchel, a German Communist functionary, the chief Nazi prosecutor remarked

* The presentation that follows, like the preceding section, is based on Wehner's memoirs and on the extensive treatment of the January conference given in the 1943 indictment of Wilhelm Knöchel, who was a member of the KPD Central Committee elected at the Brussels Conference.

that the head of the Comintern had "interpreted the political situation in a peculiar way." What he did not know was that Dimitrov had also given the German functionaries another, perhaps even more important, job: to support the Pact by "unmasking the war plans of English and French imperialism."

Once again, the Comintern and its German subsidiary had to play a double game. As for Dimitrov and several German leaders, including Ulbricht and Philipp Dengel (who had preceded Ulbricht as German representative to the Comintern), they evidently believed that the new relationship between Moscow and Berlin really meant a new chance for the KPD. Dengel even predicted that Communists working underground in Germany now no longer ran the risk of execution. Stalin, he said, would see to it that Hitler kept the persecution of Communists within bounds. Ulbricht's task, Wehner reported, was to "prevent 'primitive anti-fascism' from interfering with the 'legal possibilities' of conducting propaganda in favor of the Soviet system inside Germany."

This remark hits the nail on the head. Naturally, Stalin and his functionaries did not object to trading their friendship with Nazi Germany for German sympathy toward Bolshevik Russia or to exploiting new possibilities for Soviet propaganda in Germany. Besides, this would give the Communists in Germany who might initially have been confused by the Pact—some had been released from prisons and concentration camps after the Pact was signed—something to do, a job they could somehow understand.

"German fascism wanted to exterminate Bolshevism, but instead, the authority of the Socialist Soviet Union is steadily growing among the German people," Ulbricht wrote. "The fascists describe everything progressive and liberating as Bolshevism, and the result is that many people are trying to learn more about Bolshevism and are drawing comparisons between the barbaric conditions of Nazi rule in Germany and the Socialist victories in the land of Soviet power. . . . The peasant, who is being ruined by the fascist rule of the big capitalists over the economy, is becoming interested in the condition of the collective peasants in the Soviet Union."[20]

By far the most dangerous "deviation" in this period was what Ulbricht called "primitive anti-fascism." German Communists had to understand that while a limited degree of propagandizing in favor of the Soviet Union was now possible, it was *impermissible* to propagandize against Hitler and his Nazis. "Primitive anti-fascism" jeopardized Stalin's most important political aim: to divide Europe with Hitler. Poland had been their first booty. In November, 1939, with Hitler's approval, Soviet troops invaded Finland. A few months later, Lithuania, Latvia, and Estonia were annexed by the U.S.S.R. The alliance with the German dictator was so fruitful that under no circumstances was it to be endangered by German Communist zealots. The KPD, like the other branches of the Comintern, was told to concentrate its propaganda fire on "French and English imperialism."

Ulbricht looked for an opportunity to apply these new instructions. He found it in an article by the Social Democrat Dr. Rudolf Hilferding, "The Meaning of This War," in which Hilferding called on his political friends unequivocally and unconditionally to support victory for France and England because these two countries were fighting for the ideals of freedom. This article served as a peg for Ulbricht publicly to support the Pact and to attack England and France.

The revolutionary workers and progressive forces in Germany . . . do not want to exchange the present regime for English imperialism and British-oriented circles of German high finance and big industry. . . . They are fighting for a Germany in which the working masses truly have a say. . . .

The Hitler regime has prudently established peaceful relations with the Soviet Union, not only because supporting the English plan would victimize Germany, turn it into a satellite of English imperialism, but also because the Red Army's strength, the international power of the Soviet Union, and the sympathy German workers feel for the Socialist Soviet Union showed that such an adventure was hopeless. The ruling circles in Germany decided to reorient Germany's foreign policy.

The German Government declared itself ready to establish peaceful relations with the Soviet Union, while the aggressive Anglo-French bloc wants to wage war against the Socialist Soviet Union. The Soviet people and the German workers have a vital interest in defeating the English war plan. . . .

This is why not only the Communists but also many Social Democratic and National Socialist workers consider it their task to stand by the Pact and see that it is not violated. Whoever agitates against the friendship of the German and Russian peoples is an enemy of the German people and will be branded an accomplice of English imperialism. . . . The German people and all those nations who have been incorporated into the German state [!] are faced with this decision: to choose not English capitalism, prolongation of the war, and another Versailles, but the Soviet Union, peace, national independence, and friendship among all nations. The workers, farmers, and intelligentsia of Germany, Austria, Czechoslovakia, and Poland will be the stanchest supporters of the Soviet-German Pact and the sworn enemies of the English plan.*

---

* On August 9, 1946, the East German Communist newspaper *Neues Deutschland* carried a statement by Ulbricht explaining this article, after it had been mentioned at a Munich press conference. He said: "The criticisms in my article against certain international forces became obsolete when the Soviet Union, England, and the United States entered into an alliance, and when the English and others made great sacrifices in their fight against German fascist imperialism."

Ulbricht's article appeared in *Die Welt,* a Comintern paper published in Stockholm, on February 9, 1940. On that same day, twenty-eight men and two women were transferred to a prison in Biala Podlaska, a small Polish town, by a German SS man. They were German Communists and anti-Nazis who had fled to Soviet Russia, where they had been arrested during the purge. Now that the Stalin-Hitler Pact was in effect, the Soviet authorities had decided to return them and about 470 other German anti-fascists to Germany. Most of them died in German concentration camps.*

The Russo-German War and the National Committee for Free Germany

On Monday, June 16, 1941, Walter Ulbricht was addressing a group of German *émigrés.* During the question-and-answer period, a member of the audience remarked that foreign newspapers spoke of the possibility of a German attack on the Soviet Union, although the Soviet press had denied these reports; perhaps the speaker could give them more information? Ulbricht repeated the official denials and concluded, "These are rumors spread by provocateurs. There will be no war."[21] Six days later, German armies invaded the Soviet Union. Like Stalin, Ulbricht had until the very last

* One of the two women was Margarete Buber-Neumann, wife of the well-known KPD functionary Heinz Neumann, who died a victim of the Soviet purges. She has related her experiences in Soviet labor camps and German concentration camps in *Als Gefangene bei Stalin und Hitler (Under Two Dictators)* (Munich, 1949).

During the German-Soviet Pact, German Communist prisoners whose release had been requested by Soviet authorities were transported by the Gestapo to the Soviet Union. My attempts to turn up any documentation on the mutual exchange of prisoners during the life of the German-Soviet Nonaggression Pact—at both the Foreign Office in Bonn and the Federal Republic's Archives in Coblenz—were fruitless.

moment tried to deny that this could occur, though perhaps he had different reasons. "The German working class," he wrote in his diary, "was unable to foil Hitler's military preparations and prevent the attack on the land of Socialism. That was the worst thing of all." A few weeks later, after giving a lecture at the Soviet Military Academy, he noted, "I must confess that no lecture was ever as hard for me as this one. . . . I couldn't explain to the Soviet officers why the workers in the land of Marx and Engels, led by Thälmann's Party, had been unable to close their ranks and develop a resistance movement that would have made it impossible for Hitler to dare attack the Soviet Union."[22]

On the very day the war began, Ulbricht and Pieck were summoned by Dimitrov and told what their new task was to be. (Most German *émigrés* were deported from Moscow a few weeks after the outbreak of the war and were forcibly relocated in the distant eastern republics, the majority near Karaganda. But Ulbricht, Pieck, and other top KPD functionaries stayed in Moscow.) They were to aid the Red Army's Political Administration in processing information about German troops. They were also to propagandize prisoners of war.

Those German Communists who had survived the Moscow purge and the humiliation of the Stalin-Hitler Pact were torn between feelings of guilt and failure when their own compatriots attacked the "Soviet Fatherland." Ulbricht's diary makes this clear. But their new duties must have been a salvation: Once again, they could speak of the "implacable struggle by all anti-fascist forces" and of the defense of the Soviet Union. Defense of the Stalin-Hitler Pact was quickly forgotten.

The very first conversations between these Communist expatriates and captured German soldiers and officers showed how utterly estranged from their homeland and fellow Germans the former had become. The *émigrés* had been away from Germany for almost ten years, and though both they and the war prisoners spoke German, they nonetheless did not speak the same language. To the men in the prison camps, the Communist expatriates were dishonorable traitors. When the *émigrés* launched into Marxist speeches about the "laws of history" and the "inevitable victory of Socialism," the prisoners responded with sneers and jeers. The German flag flew over Poland, Scandinavia, and all of Western Europe; the German Army was marching on Moscow: Anyone who sided with these "lackeys of Russia" did so for material reasons alone—this was the general opinion—for instance, to get a larger food ration. And it was true: Those who promised to help in forming anti-fascist groups among the prisoners were given better rations. But Ulbricht and his friends made little progress with the captured Germans until after the Battle of Stalingrad in the winter of 1942–43, when a change in the prisoners' attitude became noticeable. More than 2,000 German officers and 91,000 soldiers of the Sixth Army had been captured during the Russian offensive; the Germans' confidence began to dwindle. The Soviets decided to take a new tack in their prison propaganda.

Toward the end of June, 1943, the prison camp newspaper *Das Freie Wort* (*The Free Word*) called on the prisoners to form a "National Committee for Free Germany."* In July, Manuilsky summoned Pieck, Ulbricht, and other German functionaries and outlined his ideas on the purpose of such

* In my account of the founding and activity of the National Committee for Free Germany, I have relied chiefly on Bodo Scheurig's excellent book (the best, I think, on the subject), *Freies Deutschland—Das Nationalkomitee und der Bund Deutscher Offiziere in der Sowjetunion, 1943–1945* (*Free Germany: The National Committee and the League of German Officers in the Soviet Union*) (Munich: 1960), pp. 34 ff.

a National Committee. There was also discussion over a flag: Ulbricht and the other Germans suggested black, red, and gold as the Committee's official colors, but Manuilsky thought these colors would not appeal to the German officers and soldiers since they were too reminiscent of the Weimar Republic. The National Committee flag should be, he argued, black, white, and red. The German Communists were horrified: The colors of Kaiser Wilhelm's Reich symbolized backward, reactionary German imperialism; but here, too, they bowed to their masters. From then on, again on orders from the Kremlin, they toned down the class-struggle theme and spoke instead of "national interests."

The manifesto that Ulbricht and other Communists wrote for the National Committee's first meeting met with vigorous protest. The small group of German officers who had agreed to work on the Committee insisted rather on a draft they had drawn up themselves. Count Einsiedel, one of the Committee's founders, wrote in his memoirs that the manifesto would have been more appropriate at a revolutionary Soldiers' Council or a German Communist Party meeting.[23] After long and violent argument between Ulbricht's expatriates and the German officers, the former managed to force through a version of their own draft that had been greatly modified to meet the officers' demands. It was solemnly proclaimed at the official founding meeting of the National Committee on July 12–13, 1943, in the quarters of the Krasnogorsk City Council.[24] The manifesto was signed by twenty-one soldiers and officers and twelve *émigrés*, among them Pieck, Ulbricht, and Wilhelm Florin, as well as the writers Johannes R. Becher, Willi Bredel, Friedrich Wolf, and Erich Weinert. Weinert was elected president of the Committee.[25] The names of national heroes—Baron vom Stein, Ernst Moritz Arndt, Clausewitz, and Count Yorck*—were solemnly evoked; so was the slogan "People and Fatherland." A "truly German" government was to be created, born of the people's struggle against the Hitler regime and dedicated to the immediate cessation of hostilities. The German armies were to be withdrawn to Germany, all conquered territories relinquished, and peace negotiations begun.

A few weeks later, part of the Committee—the soldiers and officers—moved to Lyunovo, about eighteen miles from Moscow, where it was quartered in a former rest home of the Soviet Railroad Workers Union. The civilians, under Ulbricht, worked in Moscow, where they edited the National Committee's newspaper *Freies Deutschland* (*Free Germany*) and operated a short-wave radio station. This part of the Committee operated under the official name of "Institute No. 99," at first on a side street near Arbat Square, later on Orbucha Street. Two offices were at the permanent disposal of Erich Weinert and Walter Ulbricht; the other rooms were taken up by the editorial staff of *Freies Deutschland,* among them Rudolf Herrnstadt, editor-in-chief; Lothar Bolz, later Foreign Minister of the DDR; Karl Maron, later Minister of the Interior of the DDR; and Alfred Kurella, SED expert on cultural policy.[26] The group occasionally appeared in Lyunovo to attend meetings, where Weinert presided while Ulbricht kept in the background. But the officers and soldiers soon realized that Ulbricht was the *politruk* (political officer) in charge of the entire enterprise. Einsiedel notes: "There are Communists who can handle themselves fairly well in the company of officers. But the Party *apparatchiks* like Ulbricht, with their wooden 'dialectical' monologues, are simply un-

* These four German military heroes all served in Russia, in the campaigns against Napoleon.

bearable."[27] Other officers came to the same conclusion: It was the Paris Popular Front Committee all over again.

Ulbricht ran the machine while the more conciliatory Pieck, Weinert, the other Communist writers, and several functionaries worked hard at keeping up good relations with the officers. Working in his Moscow office, Ulbricht chose the so-called front delegates and gave them their assignments. These men worked for the National Committee in various sectors of the front lines, each with several assistants. All reported directly to Ulbricht. Their major task was to broadcast the National Committee and its program to the German trenches and to see to it that as many leaflets as possible reached the German lines.*

From time to time, Ulbricht visited sectors of the front to check on the success of this propaganda; it was not great, to tell the truth. On these occasions, he would also take to the microphone and loudspeaker, and call on the German soldiers to desert to the Red Army. For National Committee propaganda had undergone a change, on Soviet orders, in 1944. Until early 1944, the slogan had been, "Let the German troops withdraw to their own national borders." But now, in the second propaganda phase of the war, the German soldiers were called on to desert to the side of the National Committee.

Ulbricht was also in charge of the schools set up behind Soviet lines where prisoners were politically "re-oriented." (Some of these indoctrinated prisoners served for a time as diversionary troops behind the German lines.) But this aspect

* Scheurig and Jesco von Puttkammer report that many thousands of leaflets, printed in Soviet front-line printing shops and thrown into the German lines, bore the mark of the National Committee, although no one in Lyunovo ever knew anything about them. (Scheurig, *op. cit.*, p. 91, and von Puttkammer, *Irrtum und Schuld—Geschichte des National-komitees 'Freies Deutschland'* [*Error and Guilt: The History of the National Committee for Free Germany*] [Berlin, 1948], pp. 75–76.)

of his work had nothing to do with the National Committee in Lyunovo, which had not the slightest say in these matters. Nor, for that matter, could the National Committee do anything about the fact that the prisoners in these schools and in the anti-fascist schools in the prison camps heard less and less of Arndt, Yorck, and Clausewitz, and more and more of Marx and Engels. Nationalist feelings had to give way to Marxism. The chief subject in the "Antifa" schools was "Marxist-Leninist Philosophy"; other subjects were: "How to Run a Meeting," "Party Tactics," "Russian History," and "Bolshevik Criticism and Self-Criticism." Former members of the Hitler Youth, now spouting Marxist slogans, became an important "cadre reserve" for the Party's future work in Germany.

The Russians began to lose interest in the National Committee, however, as the Russian troops continued their westward advance and as German unconditional surrender appeared more and more likely. The important thing now was to turn as many cooperative prisoners as possible into well-indoctrinated functionaries. Ulbricht was more at home supervising this sort of project than carrying on political discussions with German officers.

Ulbricht and other Communist Party leaders had an even more important job to do in the last months of the war. Soviet postwar policy had to be translated into guidelines for German Communists, and the *émigrés* had to be prepared for their future work in Germany. In February, 1945, Ulbricht was put in charge of a Politburo Committee formed to handle these tasks.[28] Soon after, about 150 expatriates in Moscow received orders to begin attending weekly indoctrination courses on the all-important political problems affecting their future work in Germany.

The general line enunciated in this course—where the lecturers were German Communist leaders including Pieck,

Ulbricht, Hermann Matern, and Anton Ackermann—was that German fascism had been crushed not by an internal revolution but by the military victory of the Allies: Since there had been no strong resistance movement, since the German people shared the guilt for Nazi crimes and had to be re-educated completely, a long-term occupation of the country by the anti-Hitler coalition was inevitable before they could regain their political independence. Undoubtedly, said the speakers, Nazis and other German reactionaries would try to pit the various occupation powers against each other and undermine their unity. The German Communists' main job was therefore to support the occupation powers in their efforts to eradicate fascism and militarism. They were also to see to it that all attempts to shake the unity of the four Allies—"the guarantee of victory"—were nipped in the bud.

Now, Communists in several East European countries had demanded that Socialism be established immediately; similar "left-sectarian" ideas could be expected among comrades in Germany. But dangerous tendencies would have to be fought energetically from the start: The proclamation of the proletarian dictatorship was not the immediate goal in Germany, but rather, it was the completion of the bourgeois-democratic revolution of 1848. To accomplish this, German imperialism and militarism had to be completely destroyed and various major reforms carried through. At first, political parties would not be allowed. All anti-fascists would join together in a mass organization to be called the "Bloc of Militant Democracy."

Pieck, Ulbricht, and several other German functionaries conferred at length with Dimitrov again on April 1, 1945. It is probable that at this meeting plans were made for the Politburo members' return to Germany. And it is probable that at this time it was decided that Ulbricht, accompanied

by a few others, should be the first to depart for Berlin. Those
chosen for the Ulbricht Group met with their leader several
times before the trip to discuss a number of technical details,
young Wolfgang Leonhard among them. He noted with amaze-
ment that Ulbricht did not seem to be in the least bit excited
at the prospect of soon returning to Germany: "He spoke to
us as if it were the most natural thing in the world to be returning to Germany after all these years."

Ulbricht, Germany, and the Soviet Union

In his memoirs, *The Yenan Way*, Eudocio Ravines, a one-
time Comintern functionary, describes a meeting of high-level
Comintern representatives in Moscow that took place during
the Spanish Civil War or shortly thereafter. Dimitrov was
the chief speaker. He discussed the successes and failures of
various Communist Parties and made a deprecating remark
about the work of the Communists in Germany. Pieck, Ravines
reports, leaped to his feet and replied excitedly: "You simply
can't talk that way! . . . The time has come to speak frankly
in front of all these comrades. We are sick of being told the
German Communists did not fight, that they gave up without
resistance. These things happened in order to prevent civil
war from breaking out in Germany. The Western powers
would have intervened, they would have reached the borders
of the Soviet Union, and they would have involved it in the
conflict."

Manuilsky tried to calm Pieck down, but without success.
He went on, loudly: "Moscow ordered us to give up. I want
to clarify this here in front of these comrades, because we are
being held up to ridicule and taunted with questions like:
Why didn't you fight like the Spaniards? You are the disgrace
of World Communism! . . . We Germans are not cowards,

comrades! We need not be ashamed to sit down at the same table with Spanish or Chinese Communists."

Dimitrov hastily cut the meeting short. When it resumed two days later, Pieck rose, apologized for his behavior, and retracted his remarks.

This single incident lays bare all the factors that entered into the relationship between the German Communist *émigrés* and the Russian Communists.

Communist policy in the 1930's and during the war always followed the line that best served the interests of the Soviet Union. All other viewpoints had to be subordinated to this principle, even the belief in proletarian internationalism, even the hatred of fascism and National Socialism. This policy reached its climax in the German-Soviet Nonaggression Pact and the secret agreement between Stalin and Hitler.

At the same time, the Russians placed an overwhelming burden of guilt on the German expatriates, reproaching them over and over again for having failed. Ulbricht, as far as we know, never spoke up against this, as Pieck did. But his attitude since the war as Soviet deputy in Germany shows that he, too, is afflicted with the same ambivalent feelings, and these feelings have determined his relations with Russia as well as his relations with the German people. To thousands of Germans after the war, Ulbricht passed on Moscow's accusation: "You are guilty!" "The infamous attack by Hitler's armies on the first Workers' State is the most shameful chapter in German history."[29] He demanded of the Germans precisely those things that the Soviets had demanded of all German *émigrés:* admission of overwhelming guilt, indebtedness to the Soviet Union, subordination of German interests to those of Russia, and obedience.

Ulbricht had recognized Moscow as the center of World Communism years before Hitler came to power, and he had faithfully carried out the Kremlin's orders in Germany. But the years 1933–45 altered his relations with the Soviet Union and with Germany. To begin with, Ulbricht was deprived of German citizenship in 1937 because of his alleged intention to commit high treason. Even a Communist whose loyalties are international rather than national cannot be wholly indifferent to being thus disinherited. It is rumored that Ulbricht became a Soviet citizen, but there is no proof that he did, and he himself denies it.* Basically, it is of no importance, for it is not a man's citizenship that matters, but his actions. Moreover, Ulbricht had to leave Germany in 1933; in 1937, he lost the right to call himself a German; and in 1938, he moved from Paris to the Soviet Union, where he found a "second home." But even a Communist expatriate can feel rootless. His native land, which he has been forced to leave, becomes alien to him, but he cannot free himself entirely from its hold. For his hosts, he remains the representative of a foreign land; when they denounce the injustices perpetrated there, he feels they are pointing at him. During the war, Ulbricht may have wished at times that he had been born a Russian. It is hard no longer to be part of one country and not yet of

---

* At the Berlin Foreign Ministers' Conference in 1954, Secretary of State John Foster Dulles referred to the "Soviet citizen, Ulbricht." In an interview with the East German News Agency (ADN), Ulbricht retorted: "Mr. Dulles . . . is indulging in fairy tales about me at the Conference. It is generally known that I, like many anti-fascists, was deprived of my citizenship because of 'intended high treason'—that is, because of my anti-fascist activity. Anti-fascists have never recognized this deprivation of citizenship. The Soviet authorities agreed with us that these illegal measures of the Hitler state could not be recognized, and therefore deemed it pointless for leading German anti-fascist functionaries to adopt Soviet citizenship. Mr. Dulles to the contrary, I have never received Soviet citizenship or possessed a Soviet passport. It would have been a great honor to acquire Soviet citizenship, but I never did." ("Walter Ulbricht antwortet Herrn Dulles" ["Walter Ulbricht Answers Mr. Dulles"], *Neues Deutschland*, February 4, 1954.)

another. Even the refugee—perhaps the refugee in particular—wants to belong somewhere, to be part of something.
Ulbricht, then, tried to be more Russian than the Russians,
building on his faith in the Soviet Union as the First Socialist
State, as the "Fatherland of all working people"—a faith
he had acquired decades before. Soon he began to see Germany through Russian eyes, or at least as he believed Russians saw Germany. With this transformation effected, Ulbricht
returned to his native land.

Ulbricht no doubt believed that his hatred of Germany,
and of the people who had brought death, destruction, and
suffering to the towns and villages of the Soviet Union, was
identical to the hatred felt by Soviet citizens toward Hitler's
country. But Ulbricht's hatred was more complex, and he
compensated for all the humiliation German Communists had
suffered in the Soviet Union. Holding not the Russians but
the Germans responsible, he gave vent, in his hatred, to the
bitterness of having to return as a mere deputy, of having
to rule over a satellite country. The old Communist dream of
a Soviet Germany born of victorious revolution—that dream,
too, was gone for good. The new paradox confronting Ulbricht
at the end of World War II must have deepened his hatred
even more: He despised this Hitlerite people, but only through
them could he find compensation. They were the people with
whom he had to create a Bolshevik state on German soil.

IV

The Deputy
(1945–52)

The Ulbricht Group

In the early afternoon of April 30, 1945, a plane from
Moscow landed at an airfield east of Berlin, on the Oder
River between Frankfurt and Küstrin.* Ten members of the
German Communist Party disembarked and were greeted by
a Soviet officer. They were the "Ulbricht Group": the journal-
ist and writer Fritz Erpenbeck, today Editor-in-Chief of the
East Berlin magazine *Theater der Zeit;* Gustav Gundelach,
later KPD Chairman in Hamburg and a member of the West

---

* This description of the return of the "Ulbricht Group" to Germany
and of its activity in Berlin is largely based on Wolfgang Leonhard's
vivid account in *Child of the Revolution* (Chicago: Henry Regnery,
1958).

German Federal Parliament (he died in 1962); Richard Gyptner, head of the East Berlin People's Police in 1949, East German Ambassador to Poland for several years, and now Deputy Foreign Minister; Walter Köppe, a relatively unimportant functionary who died in 1963; Wolfgang Leonhard, who fled East Germany in 1949 and is today a writer and journalist in the Federal Republic; Hans Mahle, general director of the radio network in the Soviet Occupation Zone after 1945, who fell out of favor in 1951 and is presently Editor-in-Chief of the KPD newspaper in West Berlin, *Die Wahrheit;* Karl Maron, Minister of the Interior in East Germany until 1963; and Otto Winzer, presently Deputy Foreign Minister in East Germany; in addition, a technical secretary whose name is not known.

From the airport, the Ulbricht Group resumed its homeward journey, at first in a truck and later in limousines driven by Soviet soldiers. They traveled with a constant escort of Red Army officers. Finally, they arrived at Bruchmühle, a small village in the district of Strausberg, some twenty miles east of Berlin. It was headquarters both for Colonel-General Berzarin, Soviet Commandant of Berlin, and the political staff of Marshal Zhukov's army, headed by General Galachiev. Ulbricht was immediately received by the General. The next morning he left for Berlin.

When Ulbricht returned to Bruchmühle from Berlin that evening, he called his group together for a meeting. He told them that their priority task was to establish civil borough administrations as quickly as possible, made up not only of Communists and Social Democrats, but progressive middle-class elements as well. Engineers, technicians, and skilled workers had to be found who could start up the electric-power stations and waterworks. The members of the group were to split up and take responsibility for individual boroughs. They would meet in Bruchmühle every evening, compare notes, and discuss their next move.

The following morning, the Ulbricht Group went to work. Each man carried a document signed by General Galachiev stating he represented the Central Political Administration of Zhukov's Army. The repatriates quickly set about looking for suitable men and women to serve in the new Berlin borough administrations. At first, of course, they concentrated on Communists whom they knew from the past; political officers attached to the Soviet military district command gave them lists of anti-fascists. Every evening, when they returned to Bruchmühle, Ulbricht urged them on to greater speed: The civil administrations had to be "operational" within two weeks.

A few days later, Ulbricht gave the group more detailed instructions on the "correct" political make-up of the local administrations:

We must not use Communists as mayors, except in Wedding or Friedrichshain. In working-class districts, the mayors should preferably be Social Democrats. In the middle-class sections—Zehlendorf, Wilmersdorf, Charlottenburg, etc.—we must appoint someone from the middle class—a former member of the Center, Democratic, or German People's Party. It would be best if he were an intellectual, but in any event he must be an anti-fascist, someone with whom we can cooperate. . . . As for deputy mayors in charge of food supplies, the economy, social welfare, and transport, let's pick Social Democrats who know something about municipal affairs. Anti-fascist doctors should head the health departments; qualified, non-party experts shall run the post office and communications. At least half if not more of all posts must be filled by middle-class elements or Social Democrats. . . .

And now to our comrades. The first deputy mayor, the officials in charge of personnel and education—these must be our people. You must also find reliable comrades in each district to organize the police.[1]

Ulbricht answered all questions raised by his instructions quickly and to the point: "It must look democratic, but we must have complete control."

The new Berlin city government was established in May, 1945, on this basis. The Lord Mayor, sixty-eight-year-old Dr. Werner, head of an architecture school, had as little administrative experience as his deputy, the Communist Karl Maron. Otto Winzer took charge of public education and Wilhelm Pieck's son, Artur Pieck, became chief of personnel. The new city fathers—seven of them "bourgeois," six Communist functionaries, two Social Democrats, and two non-party men —were introduced by Ulbricht to the Berlin Soviet Commandant on May 18 and officially appointed by the latter the next day.

During the second week in May, the Ulbricht Group moved from its temporary home to larger offices at Prinzenallee 80 in Berlin-Lichtenberg. Ulbricht lived and worked on the first floor, which housed the Group's offices. There he continued his daily conferences with his Party collaborators, a group that had grown in the recent weeks and now included Roman Chwalek, Ottomar Geschke, Waldemar Schmidt (later Police Chief of East Berlin), and Hans Jendretzky. Larger conferences attended by 80 to 100 officials were held every Sunday in a nearby movie theater. Although the Soviet authorities had appointed a liaison officer, Ulbricht also conferred frequently with Marshal Zhukov's representatives or with the Marshal himself at Karlshorst, where the Soviet Military Government for Germany (SMAD) had its headquarters. (Ulbricht spoke Russian, and many of the Soviet officers spoke German, but Leonhard had, on several occasions, to accompany Ulbricht to Karlshorst as his interpreter.)

More Communist *émigrés* returned to Berlin at the beginning of June—among them Paul Wandel, Fred Oelssner, and Johannes R. Becher. Ulbricht immediately closeted himself with the newcomers for long talks. Two days later, he told the members of his Group that the German Communist Party would be reborn in a few days. On June 10, the Soviet Military Government issued Order No. 2, permitting the formation of parties and trade unions in the Soviet Occupation Zone. The next morning, the German Communist party was re-established, and the activities of the Ulbricht Group came to an end.

A Deputy in the Government of Deputies

The Communist Party of Germany was now to be led by a new, sixteen-member Central Committee headed by Wilhelm Pieck. Of the sixteen, only two, Ottomar Geschke and Hans Jendretzky, had been in Germany throughout the entire period of Nazi rule. The rest—Pieck, Ulbricht, Franz Dahlem, Anton Ackermann, Gustav Sobottka, Johannes R. Becher, Edwin Hörnle, Michel Niederkirchner, Hermann Matern, Irene Gärtner (i.e., Elli Schmidt), Bernard Koenen, Martha Arendsee, Otto Winzer, and Hans Mahle—had lived out the 1930's and the war in Paris and in the Soviet Union. (Dahlem was an exception, for his main sphere of activity had been in the West European countries; in 1942, the Vichy government removed him from one of its internment camps and handed him over to the Gestapo. He was put in a concentration camp.) Any influence over KPD policy wielded by representatives of the German Communist underground was virtually excluded from the start, therefore, especially since the repatriated Committee members had close contact with the Soviet Military Government and since there was reliable evidence that the KPD's new political program was the work of the Soviet "friends."

During Hitler's twelve-year dictatorship, members of the German underground, however, had developed their own ideas on political programs. They had become unaccustomed to taking orders from the Party *apparat,* and they were self-assured. There was more that separated them from the repatriated *émigrés* than the latter realized.

One divisive issue was the attitude taken toward the occupation power. Everyone agreed that the Red Army troops were to be viewed as "liberators." But the "native" Communists were much closer to the people than the "Muscovites," and they had personally experienced or heard at first hand of the atrocities being committed by Red Army soldiers. During an Ulbricht Group Sunday meeting, a former member of the underground had already demanded that abortions for women raped by Soviet soldiers be permitted. Others had suggested that German Communists publicly dissociate themselves from the atrocities committed by the "liberating" troops. Although Ulbricht and other *émigrés* had spoken to the Soviet authorities about the rapes and the looting, they would not tolerate any discussion of these problems. Nor were they willing to discuss the problem of industrial dismantling. In short, the "Muscovite" functionaries, headed by Ulbricht, denied the local Communists the right to criticize the Soviet Union or its troops.

There were also disputes over the form the Party should take. Through illegal sources, especially Radio Moscow, a few members of the German Communist underground had learned what their Party leaders had said in exile. They now reminded them that, after 1938, the *émigrés* had repeatedly advocated a united workers' party of Communists and Social Democrats once the Nazis were defeated. Ulbricht himself had said, "Like their KPD comrades, revolutionary Social Democratic, non-party, and Christian workers are quite justified in demanding that every effort be made to create a united workers' party in Germany. . . . Experience has taught the underground fighters within the country the need to create a unified revolutionary workers' party of the German proletariat in order to carry on unremitting political activity."[2] This reasoning reflected faithfully the hopes of many KPD and SPD members who had suffered together under Hitler and had fought together against him. They were convinced that the "fraternal strife in the German workers' movement" had been one of the causes of the Nazis' rise to power. Yet, despite the promises, the German Communist Party had now been re-established without any offer of unity to the Social Democrats.

The members of the new Central Committee had a hard time explaining the contradiction. Ulbricht argued along the following lines: Fascism, he said, had radically decimated the ranks of the KPD. Unfortunately, those Communists who had survived the Gestapo terror had not been in a position to assimilate the latest developments in Marxist-Leninist thought. As for the Social Democrats, they were still infected by reformism and unable to adopt a friendly attitude toward the Soviet Union. All these difficulties, he said, would come to the surface in a united party and would weaken it. "Ideological issues" had to be straightened out before organizational unity could occur.[3]

There were sharp differences over the KPD program as well. Most of the resistance fighters believed that their long-dreamed-of goal, the proletarian dictatorship, would be set up in Germany immediately after the victory over the Nazis.

To their complete astonishment, the Party's manifesto mentioned nothing of the kind. It proclaimed instead that:

> We believe it would be wrong to force the Soviet system on Germany, because it bears no relation to Germany's present stage of development. We believe the overriding interests of the German people at present prescribe a different road—the establishment of an anti-fascist, democratic regime, a parliamentary-democratic republic, with all democratic rights and liberties for the people.[4]

The KPD veterans scanned the manifesto in vain for such old, familiar words as revolution, class struggle, and Socialism. Neither Marx nor Engels, Lenin nor Stalin, was mentioned. In answer to them, the *émigrés* argued defensively that even before World War II, they had ceased to demand the immediate establishment of "Soviet power" but had called instead for a democratic republic in Germany. Ulbricht himself had said, "The question is raised in public discussion: What guarantees are required to make further aggression by German imperialism impossible? Our answer is: The only guarantee is the victorious fight for a democratic republic."[5] But, argued the former underground workers, they had not been able to participate in the decision on this line of approach. Now that they had a chance to express themselves, however, they were harshly condemned by the *émigrés*.

In a letter to Dimitrov, Ulbricht complained that the majority of German Communists were "sectarian-minded," always talking out of turn about setting up "Soviet power." He lectured these "sectarians" like a schoolteacher and, in articles and speeches, tried to explain that the "class-consciousness" of most German workers had been destroyed under twelve years of Nazi rule. Socialism could not be built with a minority, he remarked. Besides, one had better not forget that

Germany was occupied by four powers, of which three were "capitalist." "To me, it seems rather dangerous to talk about Socialism now, because the great ideal of Socialism might be discredited by the occupation and by the terrible postwar conditions."[6] The really urgent job was not to introduce Socialism, but to build an anti-fascist, democratic society.

This view followed Soviet policy in all areas occupied by the Red Army. Stalin had adopted Lenin's theory of stages in the proletarian revolution to meet changed conditions; the bourgeois revolution was to be carried through in "administrative" fashion, thereby creating favorable conditions for the transition to Socialism.

The main blow was to be aimed not at the bourgeoisie as a whole, but at "the supporters and representatives" of fascism: monopoly capital, "the armaments plutocracy," "the most reactionary, chauvinistic, imperialistic elements of finance capital," "big landowners," and Junkers—those breeders of militarism. Basic reforms were needed to break the power of these groups and destroy fascism forever. The government bureaucracy had to be purged (state reform), the banks and giant industrial combines expropriated (economic reform), and the large landed estates confiscated (land reform).[7]

Obviously, the expropriation of the most powerful economic groups under the slogan of anti-fascism anticipated perhaps the most important stage in the proletarian revolution. For this reason, Moscow gave responsibility for the three major reforms to its most trusted agent in Germany—Ulbricht. On the Central Committee, he took charge of the departments for government, the economy, agriculture, and labor policy. Wilhelm Pieck was responsible for "general policy"; Franz Dahlem for Party organization; Anton Ackermann for cultural affairs and public education, as well as the press and

Party education—i.e., for the fourth major planned reform, educational reform.

Even before the American troops had left Thuringia, Saxony-Anhalt, and West Saxony, Ulbricht and two representatives of the Soviet Military Government left Berlin for a series of visits to the cities in what was to be the Soviet Zone—among them Weimar, Jena, Halle, and Leipzig. There, too, they made arrangements for rebuilding local civil government along the lines laid down by Moscow and already tested in Berlin. But now the less important and unpopular departments—e.g., for food supplies—were left to representatives of the three other parties that had been established in the interim—the Social Democratic Party (SPD), the Christian Democratic Union (CDU), the Liberal Democratic Party (LDP)—or to non-party men. (On July 14, 1945, at the suggestion of the Communists, the KPD, SPD, CDU, and LDP in the Soviet Occupation Zone formed a "United Front," a "coalition of Anti-fascist–Democratic parties" that would "solve the great tasks with their united forces." So-called Bloc Committees were created on all levels, comprising representatives of the four parties.) Since the Communists were determined to mask their "leading role" in this democratic-looking set-up, they devised a "deputy system": They would place a non-Communist at the head of the local government and entrust the real administrative apparatus—which the non-Communist had little time to deal with—to his deputy, a Communist. While the official leaders of the "new, democratic order" made speeches and ran from one meeting to another, Ulbricht and his collaborators established a government by deputy.

Ulbricht ruled the Communist Party on the same principle. Jovial, seventy-year-old Pieck represented the KPD to the outside world, but the deputy, Ulbricht, held the key positions.

Nor did this change with the shotgun marriage between the SPD and the KPD of East Germany in April, 1946. Pieck and Otto Grotewohl presided as co-chairmen of the new Socialist Unity Party (SED) ; Ulbricht again became deputy.

Once the deputies had put the officials who fronted for them in the limelight, they brought the extras and the bit players on stage. Their role was to demonstrate noisily in favor of measures the deputies wanted: Land reform was staged and carried out in just this way, for instance. Before the necessary decrees could be issued, the impression had to be created that large estates were being distributed among the small and middle farmers because that was what the farmers themselves had proposed.

Ulbricht continued his travels in the Soviet Zone throughout the summer of 1945, visiting small country towns and villages. He talked to mayors, farmers, and agricultural experts about all sorts of agricultural matters—delivery quotas under the Nazis, harvesting, soil fertility, etc. He also asked the farmers what they thought about breaking up the big estates. Years later, Ulbricht described one such conversation with Herr Heilemann, mayor of the village of Schlaitz:

"How do you make a living?" I asked. His answer was, "I have two hectares." "But you can't make a living or even feed a family from two hectares," was my rejoinder, to which he responded, "I know, but I also work on the estate." "What," I asked in astonishment, "you people still have landlords here?". . .

Then we went to his house and talked with him and some other peasants. "Look here," I said, "you have a very strange democracy in your village. The mayor has to work for the big landlord who gives the orders. What kind of mayor are you? What kind of village council do you have? The landlord has the economic power—the land—while he lets you hold occasional council meetings as window dressing." Comrade Heilemann agreed: "You're right, but how can we change it?" "That's simple," we advised him. "Take the landlord's property."[8]

Following Ulbricht's visits, Party functionaries would go to each of the villages and organize meetings of the local population under the slogan "Junker estates to the peasants!" It was not hard to win them over with the slogan "We want more land!" Every day, resolutions from farmers and agricultural workers calling for the break-up of the big estates poured into Berlin. A draft law to this effect had, of course, been prepared well in advance. It had been drawn up in Moscow and translated into German by Wolfgang Leonhard, then working for the KPD Central Committee. On September 3, 1945, it was issued as a decree on land reform applying to Saxony Province; the other provinces of central Germany were next in line. All estates of more than 250 hectares were expropriated without compensation, and the land was distributed among local farmers, agricultural workers, and ethnic German expellees.

On June 30, 1946, Ulbricht celebrated his fifty-third birthday. On the evening of that day, he informed the Soviet officers at Karlshorst that the major reform of the industrial economy could begin. Marshal Zhukov had already seized the property of "war and Nazi criminals" in the Soviet Occupation Zone under Order No. 124 in October, 1945; shortly thereafter, the SED faction in the four-party bloc had proposed holding a referendum in Saxony, where more than 40 per cent of the Soviet Zone's industrial output was produced, on the expropriation of the property of "war criminals and Nazi activists." The Communists were sure they could count on "Red Saxony's" traditional voting pattern to endorse the expropriation of the huge industrial enterprises. Ulbricht had taken charge of organizing the referendum and had gone to his native province to prepare for the balloting, an army of agitators accompanying him to flood Saxony's villages and towns. Where they met with resistance, the Soviet occupation forces stepped in and arrested the most stubborn opponents of the referendum.

On June 30, 1946, therefore, the SED announced that 77.7 per cent of the voters had approved the expropriation. Ulbricht declared: "The people of Saxony have lifted high the banner of peace and democratic freedom." In July and August, the five district governments in the province nationalized 45 per cent of the Soviet Zone's industrial capacity.

The Political Turning Point, 1948–49

On April 16, 1948, the teachers and pupils of the SED Party Training School in Kleinmachnow, a Berlin suburb, welcomed a very special guest: Walter Ulbricht. He was there to tell them of important changes pending in the Soviet Occupation Zone—of the sharpening class struggle in Germany, of conflicts with "reactionary elements" in both bourgeois parties, and of the "leading role" of the SED, on which greater weight had now to be placed. But these were just details in a new, general program. SED propaganda was still silent on the fact that the Soviet Zone had ended its Anti-fascist–Democratic period in 1948 and had moved into a new stage whose goal was a "People's Democracy." The building of Socialism in the image of the Soviet Union had become the main business at hand.

It had become clear immediately after the end of World War II that the alliance between the Soviet Union and the three Western powers based on their common struggle against

Nazi Germany had succumbed to postwar tensions. The divergence between the Soviet Union and its three allies over Germany's future led to the failure of the Paris Foreign Ministers' Conference in the summer of 1946 and the Moscow Conference in the spring of 1947. The possibility of German reunification through Allied agreement thereby suffered a severe blow, and the conflict of interest among the occupation powers became more glaring. The Soviet Union decided to link its zone as closely as possible to the East European bloc, while the Western powers set about tying their zones to the Western bloc. The Soviet Union's original plan to extend the "Antifascist–Democratic order" to the rest of Germany was discarded, and with it vanished all restraint in ruthlessly sovietizing its own zone.

The most important condition for building Socialism in central Germany was the transformation of the SED into a *new type* of Bolshevik Party—i.e., into a party organized along Bolshevik lines, committed to Bolshevik ideology, and unreserved in its acceptance of the Russian Communist Party's "leading role." This change came about as a direct result of the outbreak of the Soviet-Yugoslav conflict in the summer of 1948. The Kremlin wanted to prevent the other countries under its control from adopting Belgrade's independent attitude; it demanded that all the East European Communist Parties transform themselves into satellite organizations modelled on the CPSU. The SED leadership was one of the first to comply and wholeheartedly support Moscow in its conflict with Belgrade.

But turning the SED into a Bolshevik Party was needed for other reasons. The growth of the "People's Sector" in central German industry (by the beginning of 1948, 99 per cent of the mines, half of the metallurgical production, and half of power production had been nationalized), as well as the Soviet Union's desire to link its economy to the Eastern bloc, led to the introduction of a planned economy in the Soviet Zone during the summer of 1948.

The economic plan of a Communist state is a social plan as well. If the plan in the Soviet Zone was to succeed, therefore, it was imperative to implant new attitudes and new measures of prestige, to mold all spheres of life to the needs of the plan. Planning entailed putting women into the factories, establishing "Socialist competition," an "activist" (Stakhanovite*) movement, a system of prizes for productivity far above the average "norm," and last but not least, a centralized, all-embracing system of regulation and control. Without centrally directed and disciplined organization, there was no hope of attaining the goal of this planning—that is, the gradual transformation of the existing social order into a Communist society.

The Bolshevization of the Socialist Unity Party, still spared from colorless, ideological uniformity by the presence of former Social Democrats and independent old Communists, began in the summer and fall of 1948 and speeded up after the First Party Conference in January, 1949. By then, the *History of the Communist Party of the Soviet Union* had become the basic text for Party education, to be mastered by each and every SED member through "self-study." Ulbricht proclaimed the slogan of the hour: "Learning from the Soviet Union means—learning how to conquer." Party members and functionaries who refused to submit unconditionally to Bolshevization and to the cult of the Soviet Union and Stalin

* In 1935, the Russian coal miner Alexei Stakhanov set what was then a new production record, and new records were soon chalked up in other industries and in agriculture. As a result, work norms for average workers were repeatedly raised. The East German "Stakhanov" was also a miner, named Adolf Hennecke, who fulfilled his norm by 380 per cent on October 13, 1948. —TRANSLATOR'S NOTE.

were removed from their jobs and from the Party—especially many Social Democrats, some of whom were persecuted as "Schumacher agents"* and arrested, unless they managed to escape to the West. Organizational specialists, incapable of independent ideas but therefore all the more ready to accept and execute orders in a disciplined way, advanced within the Party; they were functionaries without personal distinction but with a feeling for power and tactics, devoid of moral scruples but willing to work very hard and subordinate their personal lives to the Party's demands. Ulbricht was their model and leader. By 1950, the post of Party chairman, held jointly by Pieck and Grotewohl, was abolished. At the Third Party Congress in July of that year, Ulbricht became General Secretary of the Central Committee of the SED. The deputy had now officially assumed power.

The General Secretary

When the initial postwar reforms in the Soviet Zone had been completed, the Soviet Union put Ulbricht in charge of economic planning. Together with economists, Party functionaries, and Soviet planning experts, Ulbricht drafted a brief transition plan for the first half of 1948 and a two-year plan for 1949–50. A Commission chaired by Ulbricht met again in 1950 to prepare a five-year plan for the period from 1951 to 1955. Ulbricht had arrogated to himself the task of reporting on economic policy and plan fulfillment to Party Congresses and Conferences. Indeed, even in his inaugural speech as General Secretary, Ulbricht dealt with the German Democratic Republic's future economic policy. He predicted that in the years immediately ahead, the D.D.R. would attain

* Kurt Schumacher, then head of the SPD in Western Germany. —Translator's Note.

"a tempo of industrial development" no capitalist country would be able to match. The living standards of the East German populace would soon far surpass those of "imperialist Germany"—where unemployment and economic chaos were permanent conditions.

The Bolshevization of the Soviet Zone, the SED's naked claim to the "leading role" in East Germany, and the predictable consequences of its planning placed the non-Communist parties in a dilemma. Their representatives, who could neither stop nor derail "the train of Socialist progress" because of the occupation, tried at least to slow it down. But Ulbricht had already "planned" how to break this resistance.

The bourgeois parties, he said, had to undergo a "process of clarification." The "old reactionary forces" saw their positions threatened by the forced sharpening of the class struggle; now they had to disappear from political life. Christian Democrats and Liberal Democrats who were ready to cooperate in building Socialism would continue to be tolerated, but the bourgeois front had to be split apart.

Two more officially non-Communist parties were founded for this purpose in 1948 with the help of the Soviet occupation power: the National Democratic Party (NDP) and the Democratic Peasant Party. Many functionaries of the NDP, which specialized in recruiting former Nazis, came out of the National Committee for Free Germany and the wartime "antifascist" schools in the Soviet Union. The chairman of the Peasant Party and many of his collaborators were "disempowered" by the SED. Under these conditions, it is not surprising that representatives of both new parties almost always adopted the SED position at meetings of the Bloc Committees. It was exactly the same in the regional parliaments,* where

* Another Ulbricht reform had been to dissolve the five German provinces in the Soviet Zone and replace them by fifteen regional districts.

the Communists were also supported by the mass organizations that were permitted to enter candidates for election. (Their candidates were frequently SED members.)*

Ulbricht then declared that Nazi members and activists, many of whom were "taking part in the building of Socialism," were no longer the "main danger." That unpleasant distinction was now reserved for the CDU and LPD politicians who represented "monopolists and bankers" and who had sneaked into their parties in order to protect their employers' interests. "Coercive measures" would not be taken against them, but mass meetings had to be organized at which "certain people" would be forced to account publicly for their "negative propaganda." Afterwards, they would be publicly enlightened on the meaning of democracy. "It would be ridiculous if we could not win against them under these democratic conditions."[9]

Representatives of the bourgeois parties who continued to engage in public polemics were subject to cross-examination by SED functionaries. Inevitably, there was no agreement between the accused man and his Communist prosecutors on the nature of democracy. If the accused decided to tell the truth, then he had to admit he was opposed to Soviet policy and the Soviet occupation, but these were grounds for further indictments. Many of the best men who had founded and built the middle-class parties in the Soviet Zone lost their government jobs, were arrested, or fled to West Germany. From 1950 to 1952, 892 CDU members alone were sentenced to long prison terms, including hard labor. "Our country's vital interests and the defense of peace," Ulbricht declared, "make it

---

* In addition to the five parties, the following mass organizations are now represented in the People's Chamber of the D.D.R.: Free German Trade-Union Federation, Free German Youth, Democratic League of Women, Farmers' League for Mutual Aid, and the Cultural League.

impossible for us to allow the representatives of a suicidal policy . . . to be active in the parties of the anti-fascist–democratic bloc."[10]

Spokesmen of the middle class and many non-Communist workers and white-collar employees fought against the trend from positions that soon were lost to them. They had little to hope for from a Communist occupation power. Still, they may have asked themselves, was there not the possibility that Moscow might shift its support from one wing of the German *Communists* to another?

But the scope for differing views had been limited from the beginning, and it grew smaller with each passing year. Once the conflict with Yugoslavia had started, Moscow recognized how dangerous national Communist tendencies in its satellite countries could become. It abandoned its original tolerance of varying national conditions while pursuing its own interests. The one serious difference that might now arise in a Communist Party leadership would be over the most successful way of sovietizing the country. Much depended on which group or individual had the best connections with Moscow or with the Soviet military command—not only so as to be able to find out what views prevailed in those quarters, but also so as to be the first to brief *them* on the current local situation.

According to the original division of labor in the SED Central Secretariat,* co-chairmen Pieck and Grotewohl were supposed to have conducted the necessary negotiations with the Soviet Military Government in Karlshorst. Ulbricht managed to take over that department of the Party apparatus too. With few exceptions, every functionary of the SED Central

---

* The "Central Secretariat" disappeared with the organizational change in the SED. A separate Politburo and Secretariat were established along the lines of the Russian Communist Party.

Secretariat who wished to contact a Soviet representative had to get Ulbricht's permission. And yet, or partly because of this fact, Ulbricht at first had trouble in persuading the Party leaders to accept his views. There had been violent clashes at meetings of the Central Secretariat, and quite often decisions had had to be modified. The differences between former Social Democrats and Communists had crystallized in the conflicting attitudes of Ulbricht and Grotewohl and the discord between Ulbricht and Max Fechner, a former SPDer who also served as a deputy chairman. Ulbricht and Grotewohl had often been hard put to conceal their dislike for each other. As early as the summer of 1946, Grotewohl had told a friend that this fellow Ulbricht was "dangerous."[11] He saw through Ulbricht, but he was no match for him. For Ulbricht had learned how to commit moral blackmail against Grotewohl. He knew that the Nazi seizure of power had left Grotewohl with a deep feeling of guilt. Ulbricht shamelessly exploited this feeling that the democratic forces had failed and shared responsibility for Nazi Germany. He learned how to shake Grotewohl's self-confidence with statements like: "Do you once more want to take the opportunistic Social Democratic road that led to Fascism?" Or, "You failed once—do you want to fail again?" And Ulbricht used the same method on representatives of the middle-class parties.

Grotewohl resisted frequently at first. So did Fechner, who, being experienced in municipal politics, also opposed Ulbricht's idea that only a highly centralized administrative apparatus could serve the interests of the SED. But a number of indiscretions and his loose tongue brought Fechner into conflict with his old SPD friends as well and in 1950, he was forced to vacate his place in the Party leadership.*

---

* In the summer of 1953, Fechner was expelled from the SED and arrested as "an enemy of the Party and State." As Minister of Justice,

Ulbricht's efforts systematically and ruthlessly to expand his power and to impose his views on the SED quickly aroused the hostility of other former SPD functionaries in the Party leadership. Their dislike was intensified by the fact that Ulbricht often presented as his own proposals that had actually originated with the Soviet Military Government.

Did Ulbricht have any serious rival among the Party leaders? Certainly not among the former Social Democrats; only veteran Communists who had unusually good relations with the occupation power might have posed a threat. To guard against such a person, Ulbricht brought every possible position that might be important in a struggle for power under his control. Paul Merker, an old Communist, and the former Social Democrat Helmut Lehmann, for example, were supposedly in charge of the Agricultural Division of the Central Secretariat. Ulbricht worked directly, therefore, with the General Secretary of the Farmers' League for Mutual Aid, Kurt Vieweg; finally, he managed to have the subdivision for cooperatives (collective farms) shifted from the Agricultural to the Economic Division, for which he was responsible.

Like Stalin in the early and mid-1920's, Ulbricht diligently cultivated the Party bureaucracy. The division heads of the Central Secretariat quickly fell under his influence, and Ulbricht arranged to preside over all their weekly meetings. When he finally became General Secretary, a clan of devoted Ulbricht supporters were already working for him in the leadership and in the subordinate Party bureaus.

By 1950, independent-minded, ex-Social Democrats were virtually no longer represented in the SED Politburo—with

---

he had written in an article after the June, 1953, uprising that the D.D.R. Constitution guaranteed the right to strike and that no one would be held accountable for taking part in a strike. Fechner was released from prison in 1956 and re-admitted to the SED in 1958.

the exception of Grotewohl. The test of whether the General Secretary could rule unchallenged by Communist rivals was now inevitable.

Pieck, who had tried to act as a mediator in his post as SED Chairman, continued to try, from his new office as President of the "Republic," to strike a balance between the different tendencies. There was no personal conflict between his ambitions as Head of State and Ulbricht's. Apart from Hermann Matern, head of the SED Control Commission, who had supported Ulbricht from the start and who recognized his authority, the other Moscow exiles in the Politburo—Anton Ackermann, Fred Oelssner, Elli Schmidt, Wilhelm Zaisser, and Rudolf Herrnstadt—had no great affection for Ulbricht, but they saw no point in a struggle for power with a man who had enjoyed the Soviets' confidence in Moscow and who had been chosen to be their key man in Germany. Accordingly, they did not challenge Ulbricht's special position but fought him at first on individual issues only.

Ackermann, who in 1946 had written a thesis on "Germany's Special Road to Socialism" at the Soviets' behest, had had to engage in "self-criticism" during the crisis with Yugoslavia, and he was pushed aside more and more in the Party leadership by Oelssner. This sly, skilled, and intelligent Party ideologist, trained in dialectics and equipped with theoretical analyses, was anathema to Ulbricht's typical *apparatchik* anti-intellectualism. Ulbricht understood, of course, that people like Oelssner were indispensable, but he could barely conceal his contempt for this "overly subtle theoretician." In return, Oelssner let it be known that the General Secretary was not to be taken seriously when it came to "theoretical questions."

The men with the best personal ties with the Russian Communist Party, Herrnstadt and Zaisser, both exceptionally in-

telligent, showed little ambition at first to Party leadership.
Both were considered *éminences grises* operating in the background. Zaisser had become Minister of State Security in
1950, and he was primarily interested in keeping Ulbricht
out of his Ministry's activities. He was known in the Party
apparatus as "the secretive one," but those who knew him
were impressed by his independence and intelligence. He
was very much respected by those who had fought in the
Spanish Civil War, where he had been known as General
Gómez. But even the functionaries who esteemed him and who
were not Ulbricht's followers believed it impossible to groom
him as a counter-candidate to Ulbricht because of the inherent unpopularity of his job. Herrnstadt, Editor-in-Chief of
the SED newspaper *Neues Deutschland,* was also an unlikely
candidate. The Party functionaries did not care for his cold
and cynical intellectuality, particularly since he had little use
for yes-men and did not hide his contempt for them.

Next to Ulbricht, Franz Dahlem held the most important
posts in the Politburo. He was in charge of organization and
personnel within the SED and, above all, responsible for
work with the KPD in West Germany. He, too, could count
on the sympathies of the Spanish Civil War veterans and
those functionaries who were repelled by Ulbricht and the
Moscow *émigrés,* for Dahlem belonged with the "Western
émigrés" and former concentration-camp prisoners. The
functionaries knew, furthermore, that he had never come to
terms with Ulbricht. There had been objective differences
and personal friction between them at the end of the 1920's
and in the 1930's, and these had continued after the war.
They also disagreed in their appraisal of the situation in
West Germany. Dahlem, because of his close cooperation
with KPD functionaries there, viewed conditions in the Fed-

eral Republic more realistically than Ulbricht, and warned against illusions.

Dahlem was aware that Ulbricht was waiting for a chance to "ground" him. But Pieck, in particular, gave him strong backing; he valued Dahlem and used him as a counterweight to Ulbricht. Besides, Dahlem profited from a principle the Soviets followed in all their satellites: They made sure that they had a chief agent—in Germany, Ulbricht—but they let it be known they could shift their favor any time. A deputy was not ever supposed to feel secure, had always to be conscious of his dependence, and had always to earn the trust placed in him. Moreover, it was necessary to maintain potential new leadership teams, "dark horses" in reverse. For a long time, Grotewohl was a dark horse of this kind, and it is probable that Dahlem was too.

In May, 1953, Ulbricht had his first chance to drive his adversary out of the Party leadership. Among other things, he accused Dahlem of having aided the "American spy" Noel H. Field in his attempts to settle in the Soviet Zone or Czechoslovakia. After 1945, Dahlem, in other words, had "shown complete blindness toward the efforts of imperialist agents to penetrate the Party." Field, who the Communists were later forced to admit had not been an American agent and whose name played an important part in the trials of Laszlo Rajk in Hungary and Traitscho Kostov in Bulgaria, was now linked to Dahlem and to other functionaries of the SED whom Ulbricht wished to discredit. The Soviet acquiescence in this plot was one of Ulbricht's greatest triumphs. He had eliminated his most dangerous rival in the Party leadership.*

* Dahlem's "rehabilitation" occurred by stages. In 1955, he was made head of the Division for Science and Research in the State Secretariat for Higher Education. He was readmitted to the SED Central Committee in February, 1957.

Ulbricht's Method of Work

Until the end of the 1950's, the Politburo met every Tuesday in East Berlin's Unity House, headquarters of the SED Central Committee.* The offices of Politburo members working in the Party *apparat,* as well as the Politburo's meeting room (known as the Small Conference Hall), were located on the third floor. Soldiers of a State Security Guard regiment protected the whole building and particularly the third floor. A visitor seeking admission to Unity House needed a pass and an appointment with a Central Committee functionary; he had to hand over his identification papers and submit his briefcase to inspection; he went through another check at the entrance to each floor.

Ulbricht prepared the weekly agenda for the Politburo meetings. Proposals dealing with important affairs had to be turned in ahead of time, along with detailed explanations, a ruling that applied to Ministers and State Secretaries, Central Committee department heads, as well as Politburo members. As a result, forty to sixty items would frequently accumulate on the agenda for the next meeting, sometimes more—several hundred typewritten pages that would have to be copied and distributed to the Politburo members. At a routine meeting, for example, additional materials requested by a Minister would be granted, a Justice Ministry proposal on sentences to be imposed in a political trial would be approved, plans for schools and universities would be surveyed, theater and city construction plans would be approved; new uniforms for the army and police would be inspected; and still to come

* This account is in large part based on Fritz Schenk, *Im Vorzimmer der Diktatur* (*In the Dictator's Anteroom*) (Cologne: 1962), pp. 237 ff So far, no member of the SED Politburo has fled to the West.

were the "big" questions—changes in the political line or in foreign policy.

The material for each Politburo meeting was supposed to be ready by the preceding Saturday afternoon, but its distribution was often delayed and many proposed decisions did not reach the top functionaries until Sunday or even Monday —that is, only a day before the meeting. There frequently may have been technical reasons for this delay, but it meant that Ulbricht had the advantage over his colleagues every time, for he was able to examine and work on the documents for several days, while the other Party leaders had to crowd their review of the material into weekends that were filled with meetings or demonstrations. No one was in a position to adopt a clear-cut point of view on each proposal offered at the meetings, and consequently, each official read only the material falling within his jurisdiction, neglecting the other questions. But Ulbricht read everything.

Heinz Lippmann, a former high Free German Youth official, has described a Politburo meeting in the early 1950's:

> At the start of the meeting, Ulbricht would ask: "Does anyone have any objections to the agenda?" Most of the time, there were none. . . . Then Ulbricht would read the first item, e.g., "spring planting," recommend some changes in the proposal, which would be recorded, and then ask, "Are there other suggestions?" Since no one besides the Politburo member whose department was directly concerned with the question had read the proposal, there was usually no discussion, and a decision would be made that agreed with Ulbricht's original opinion.

The Politburo came alive only when the General Secretary was absent. Of course, nothing important would be decided, but there was genuine discussion. Some members would try to raise questions on matters where they believed Ulbricht had made the wrong decision. In 1953, for example, Zaisser and Herrnstadt used the General Secretary's absence to focus attention on catastrophic conditions in the semi-military organization Dienst für Deutschland (Service for Germany), which was dissolved soon thereafter. Pieck and other Party officials wanted to see for themselves the conditions of some of the Service for Germany camps; while doing so, they learned that units of the East German Army were equipped with Soviet tanks—something even Pieck had not known about. Matern, usually so compliant, remarked sarcastically, "Let's hope Walter tells us if we find ourselves at war."

Ulbricht was not satisfied with making all the decisions in the Politburo: He also worked hard at cutting down its authority. Every day, he summoned officials to his office to tell them of decisions that he did not report to the Politburo. Lippmann has described one of Ulbricht's typical days:

> 9–11 A.M.: conference with the Minister and Department Heads of the Agricultural Ministry; 11 A.M.–12 noon: conference with Gustav Robelen, SED Central Committee Department Head for Army and State Security, and the head of Political Administration for the People's Army, on problems of political work in the army; noon–3 P.M.: conference with the heads of the Democratic League of Women, during which lunch is served; 4–6 P.M.: report by Secretary of Free German Youth on current campaigns; 6–7 P.M.: reports by Gluckauf and Verner on some problems of work in West Germany; conversation with Joos on political aspects of personnel problems. (Ulbricht was always very thorough on this problem since it involved his own method of picking and training personnel.) Around 9 P.M., as a rule, he would talk with the Soviet Zone authorities, although he usually called them several times a day. . . . In the evening, he generally met with Central Committee Department heads and dictated specific instructions connected with that day's conferences.

Ulbricht usually had six to eight conferences a day at which basic problems of policy, the economy, culture, etc., were taken up. . . . During these meetings, decisions were made that frequently never reached the Politburo. At these conferences, Ulbricht always had notes prepared on questions he considered important. First, the invited functionaries would report, then Ulbricht would explain how he viewed future developments, and finally, he would give concrete directives on what he wanted done.

The meetings often lasted longer than planned and the Ministers, heads of mass organizations, and others waiting to be called would have to sit idle for hours, outside Ulbricht's office.

Lippmann continues:

Ulbricht's work load amazed even his enemies. We kept asking ourselves, How can Ulbricht keep it up? —twelve or fourteen, sometimes sixteen, hours a day, from one meeting to another without any sign of fatigue!

But a close look at Ulbricht's method of working shows that it was not so impressive. For apparently he received general directives from the Soviets; his skill lay in applying these instructions to specific areas. . . .

More than once I had the following experience: While the heads of the Free German Youth were kept waiting, Ulbricht would be meeting with Hoffmann, Dölling, and the Army leaders. As this first meeting ended, the two groups would be thrown together, and we would learn what had been decided. Then we would be called in, and we would hear the same things the Army people had been told, slightly altered to fit the situation in the FDJ. When we left, economic experts and trade-union officials would already be waiting outside. The next day, we learned from them that they had received the same basic instructions.

SED functionaries who from time to time reported in person to the Politburo were amazed by Ulbricht's rudeness toward his colleagues. When Oelssner, for example, would begin a theoretical analysis, Ulbricht would cut him off with remarks like, "Stop talking, Fred!" or "Shut up!" He called Dahlem a "senile fool" who no longer did any real work.

Ulbricht frequently submitted questions that should have been handled in the Politburo to another body—the Central Committee Secretariat. The Secretariat was supposedly responsible for transmitting directives to the Party *apparat*, while the Politburo was supposed to make the major political decisions. But Ulbricht had not yet succeeded in staffing the Politburo with his own people, as he had the Secretariat, where a considerable number of young officials were devoted to him and unquestioningly accepted his authority. Among them were: Willi Stoph, Secretary for the Economy and Special Deputy for Defense (now President of the D.D.R.); Hans Lauter, Secretary for Culture; the intelligent and tractable Hermann Axen, later Editor-in-Chief of *Neues Deutschland;* and Karl Schirdewan, co-opted to the Secretariat in 1953. We might also add the Secretary for Agriculture at the time, Kurt Vieweg; Paul Verner, who is now Berlin Party Secretary; and the veteran office director of the Politburo and Secretariat, Otto Schön. Erich Honecker, FDJ Chairman and alternate member of the Politburo since 1950, was also part of this group.

By 1950, Ulbricht seems to have made a deep impression on the younger Party officials. Although they did not like him, they accepted him with a mixture of fear and respect, and tried hard to do the General Secretary's bidding and save themselves from attack. They knew that his talent was often nothing more than a gift for reducing policy to a few simple generalizations, but they also recognized the advantages a politician can reap by prudently approaching difficult problems with a few standard formulas.

Many years after his flight from East Germany, Lippmann tried to describe the impression Ulbricht then made on him:

> One thing is sure: Ulbricht is completely self-confident! Completely! You had to be there when he ridiculed somebody! A cynical man. If you said something, tried to explain something to him—he'd knock it down with one sentence, a few banal words. For example, we made an extensive analysis of Social Democracy in West Germany, a study based on hundreds of individual reports. So we got together, Ulbricht, Dahlem, and I. I reported. And then Ulbricht interrupted— the words stuck in my throat.

Nor did these young Party officials relax when they met Ulbricht socially. On the contrary, they felt inhibited and unsure of themselves. Lippmann tells of a birthday party at Honecker's to which all Secretaries of the FDJ Central Council were invited and to which he went in a rather gay mood. Ulbricht arrived at about 11 P.M.: "Erich [Honecker] accepted his congratulations, we others greeted the Party chief in the humble and restrained manner we thought proper." Everyone seemed "paralyzed," although Ulbricht tried to be friendly and not spoil the festive mood. "We tried to look as if we had something to do at the far end of the room from Ulbricht. . . . Everyone tried to find a reason to leave. Yet all of us were loyal Stalinists, and if someone had asked us at that moment: 'Why are you avoiding Ulbricht?' not one of us would have been able to explain." Undoubtedly, the FDJ leaders were victims that evening of the SED chief's well-known inability to establish personal contact; still, it is significant that it never dawned on them to treat Ulbricht as "a comrade among comrades." Even at that convivial birthday gathering, he remained the feared and respected General Secretary.

From 1950 to 1953—more exactly, until Stalin's death in March, 1953—Ulbricht revealed to those around him the factors so valuable to his past and future career: The Soviets trusted no one more than him; none of his colleagues could claim greater experience in the Party apparatus; his talents and long training enabled him continuously to expand his power; through intrigue and ruthlessness, he kept ousting other veteran *apparatchiks* from the center of power; and he cautiously filled one post after another with younger men who would pose no threat for him and who were well aware of their dependence on him.

There were top functionaries, of course, who could match Ulbricht in one or another field, but as General Secretary, he had advantages over them all. His passion for work, his methodical approach and his staying power also favored him greatly. When others, exhausted by endless meetings, listened with only half an ear to what was going on, ready to yield out of sheer weariness, he would push his view all the more stubbornly and win another round. To be sure, he was particularly responsible for certain spheres—the economy and government administration; there were others he took special pleasure in supervising—the youth movement, sports, the armed forces; but unlike the other SED leaders, he concerned himself with everything. Stalin had found an ideal deputy.

Ulbricht: The Personal Story

One day in September, 1962, a London *Daily Herald* reporter, Dennis Newson, rang the doorbell at Geisslerstrasse 2, Leipzig. A simple nameplate next to the bell bore the inscription *Ulbricht*. The door was opened by a red-haired woman with a friendly expression, thin to the point of gauntness. She was the divorced wife of the present Chairman of the D.D.R.'s Council of State.

Martha Ulbricht, just a few years younger than her former husband, still lives in the same simple two-and-a-half–room apartment into which the young couple moved after their marriage. She subsists on her old-age pension and the rent of her lodger. Her only daughter, Dorle, is married and lives with her husband and two sons in the Federal Republic. Mrs. Ulbricht visited them frequently before the Berlin Wall went up. But this is no longer possible, and the old woman spends almost every evening alone watching television. She often sees Ulbricht on the screen. "I do not like his beard," she said to Newson. "I would not let him keep it if he were still my husband." Otherwise, she had become rather indifferent to the prominent man. "I feel nothing any more. I see him standing there, and then he is gone, and I go to bed."

The young Communist Martha Hauk had had a completely different idea of what her life would be like when she married Comrade Ulbricht in 1920. When Newson asked her forty years later if she ever would have imagined then that her husband would someday build the hated Wall and send his armed People's Police out to kill, she remained silent, and then hesitantly replied, "Those things are bad. I know we both would never have thought them possible. But times have changed. A lot of things have happened in the world which we both did not think were possible. Please do not ask me to go on. I am not in politics. I was the daughter of a piano-maker and I thought I had married a carpenter. . . . I have not spoken about the past for many years, and it is easy to get upset."[12]

Her husband went to Jena in 1921 and later to Berlin and

Moscow. He wrote to her from time to time, rarely came home, and when he did, only for a few days or even hours. Martha Ulbricht found a job as a seamstress with the Breitfeld Company of Leipzig, and her husband sent her money regularly. Shortly before the Reichstag fire, Ulbricht came home once more and picked up his belongings. The Gestapo showed up immediately after and searched the house. Mrs. Ulbricht rented a room to a young Jewess who later emigrated; she had to support herself and her daughter from then on without help. She was almost terrified when she heard of her husband's return after the war. "I had thought I would never see him again." But there was no change in her life.

Relations with women have never played an important part in Ulbricht's life. But at the end of the 1920's, he established intimate ties with a young French Communist, Rose Michel. She lived in Germany at the time, left the country when Ulbricht emigrated, and for some years after World War II, served as Berlin correspondent for the French Communist newspaper *L'Humanité*. No one knows exactly when they met; their separation probably occurred in 1934–35. Ulbricht never talked about his private life, and although there was gossip in the KPD "about everything and everybody," as an old woman Communist put it, he managed to steer clear of all gossip by his cold and uncivil manner.

Ulbricht met his present wife, Lotte, before 1933. She is ten years younger than her husband and comes from a Rixdorf worker's family.[13] The father died early and the mother then went back to her village and took over a small farm. In 1963, when she was almost 90, she said, "if I were twenty years younger, I'd be a member of a cattle-breeding brigade on a cooperative."

Lotte's older brother, Bruno—sent back by the Soviet Union into Nazi Germany for illegal work: He was quickly caught and executed—had been responsible for bringing his sixteen-year-old sister into the Free Socialist Youth just before she finished high school. As an eighteen-year-old office clerk, Lotte Kühn joined the KPD at the end of 1921. A little later, the Communist Youth League sent her to Moscow for a year's training in the apparatus of the Communist Youth International. She worked for the Party until 1933 in Berlin-Neukölln in a KPD factory cell and as a deputy in the District Municipal Council of Berlin-Friedrichshain. She apparently earned her living as a secretary in the Central Committee of the KPD.

It is not known when she married her first husband, Erich Wendt, now Secretary of State in the D.D.R.'s Ministry of Culture.* She accompanied Wendt to the Soviet Union in 1932, where he became assistant director of the Foreign Languages Publishing House in Moscow. Wendt, too, seems to have had trouble during the great purge. He lost his job and went to Engels, on the Volga, later to Siberia. Lotte apparently remained in Moscow. It was rumored in *émigré* circles that Wendt had left his wife and been arrested. One of Ulbricht's associates in the last years of the Weimar Republic says that even then, Comrade Lotte Kühn greatly admired the Berlin District Secretary. When Ulbricht spoke, "she sat and stared at him as if he were God-knows-what." The two completely sober, unsentimental people got along well together.

In 1938, after Ulbricht had moved from Paris to the Soviet capital, he and Lotte Kühn settled down together in a room at the Hotel Lux. His former friend, Rose, occupied a garret in the same hotel. Lotte cooked for Walter, looked after his things, and served as his secretary. After the war—they married in May, 1951, as soon as Ulbricht got his divorce—they

---

* Since the end of 1963, Wendt has conducted the negotiations with the West Berlin Senate about entry permits to East Berlin.

lived in a simple one-family house on Majakowski Ring in Berlin-Niederschönhausen.

Majakowski Ring was located in a fenced-off area known as the "little town," which was barred to ordinary citizens and guarded by security troops. Most of the SED élite lived there. Not all of the houseowners had been dispossessed, and those who rented out to the newcomers received rather high rents from the regime. And the new tenants took good care of the property.*

A black, white, and gold sentry-box stood at the Ulbrichts' garden gate, in front of which an armed soldier paced back and forth. The house had about six rooms. There was a room in the basement for the guard and a chauffeur. The street floor was taken up by a library and dining room. According to former SED functionaries, the furnishings were "very middle-class," verging on the vulgar. The library contained a couch with a green plush cover, a desk at the window, bookshelves along the walls, and cabinets with glassware and bric-a-brac. The room looked like the parlor of a foreman or small businessman.† The dining room gave the same impression.

The Ulbrichts had a maid, but evidently Mrs. Ulbricht prepared the evening meal herself. The food was plain but good: cold cuts, Italian salad, scrambled eggs, fried potatoes, a veal cutlet, beer and vodka. (Ulbricht does not smoke or permit smoking, and seldom drinks alcohol.) When trusted comrades visited him on the weekends or late at night for a discussion, their General Secretary might receive them in a

---

* Ulbricht and the other members of the élite later moved to a newly built residential complex near Wandlitz.

† Heinz Lippmann and the former Deputy Chairman of the West German KPD, Kurt Müller, visited Ulbricht at the house on Majakowski Ring and later described how it was furnished. I have drawn mainly on Lippmann's written report.

cardigan sweater and plaid slippers. Then he gave the appearance of a decent craftsman living in a small house built with the money he had saved. Lotte fitted into this picture admirably, with her kitchen apron and her "Will you please stop the politics and come to dinner?" When asked by East German journalists what her husband did in his leisure time, she replied that they loved to go walking together, listen to good music, and read good books. It is also rumored that Ulbricht still likes to engage in sports. He plays table-tennis with his wife, is a good swimmer, skis, and does his calisthenics every morning.

Ulbricht's second marriage has been childless, but in the first postwar years he and his wife adopted an orphan named Beate. When Ulbricht played with the little girl, he lost his rigidity, caressed and fondled the child, gave her piggy-back rides, spoke baby-talk, and was quite relaxed—even when others were present.

During the first years after the war Lotte had charge of the reception area outside her husband's office at SED Party headquarters. She then developed greater ambitions and attended the Central Committee's Institute for Social Science; her fellow-students often joked about the trouble she had grasping ideas.[14] Her field is "Work with Women"; she is a member of the Party's Women's Committee and has been decorated "in recognition of her outstanding achievements in developing the women's movement."

Once he leaves his personal surroundings, the "private" Ulbricht changes radically. Wolfgang Leonhard, describing a party that Ulbricht attended, remarked, "The affair was going along nicely; most of us were dancing or talking. But Walter Ulbricht sat in a corner with two or three functionaries from the Party's Organizational Department. The only subject was: 'We'll put *a* here, take *b* out of there, replace *x*, pull *y* out of Erfurt and send *z* to Jena.' "[15]

Other Party leaders had the same impression of him when he spent a weekend with them at the Seehaus, a castle on a small lake near Berlin which had been converted into a resort for members of the SED Central Committee Secretariat, and where each member had a weekend room. Dahlem, with his panama hat and wrinkled trousers, liked to spend his time catching crayfish; others preferred playing cards. Their wives did a lot of walking and gathered mushrooms. But Ulbricht often had his colleagues join him in visits to the farm nearby that provided them with food, to examine the silos and find out how the crops were doing.

Ulbricht still finds it hard to forget about his work and relax, for the old Ulbricht, just like the young one, suffers from an inability to communicate with other people. Now, as in his youth, he tries desperately in his private life to hide this severe handicap by talking endlessly about his work. In the immediate postwar years, he could excuse himself by saying there was no time for pleasure. Later, when he felt the need to be not only respected but admired and loved as well, he would try—in a comically helpless way—to joke with other people and act in a relaxed and natural fashion. These attempts at camaraderie were usually failures. At one party, Lippmann reports, Ulbricht resorted to an uninterrupted monologue. "He spoke of youth's happy years, acting as if politics were farthest from his mind. He asked that the dancing resume, and that no notice be taken of him. He even danced with some of the young girls and matrons, proposed a game of forfeits, and gave one of the girls a friendly kiss on the cheek. But the atmosphere did not improve. It was torture for everybody present."

Ulbricht may be guilty of political crimes, but his private

life is his own. His marital history is no different from that of many other public figures whose wives did not "develop intellectually and politically" and who had to make way for more understanding, usually younger and more attractive, women. Moreover, Ulbricht did not get rich in his job. He, the first citizen of the SED state, lives like a petty-bourgeois *arriviste*.

Still, Ulbricht's private life is politically revealing and important in that it disproves the notion that he is a demonic man. He is merely a politically dangerous, spiritually crippled and therefore pitiable, petty-bourgeois—one of those petty-bourgeois whom the political disturbances of our time have put into positions of power and who have abused that power.

V

Crises
(1953—58)

A Conflict and Its Consequences

At the beginning of 1953, several dozen high Party and government functionaries of the D.D.R. met in a room of the SED Central Committee. There was trouble in East Germany. The people were grumbling. Potatoes, meat, and coal were scarce; in fact, there were shortages of everything. The number of persons fleeing the Soviet Zone had risen sharply since the previous summer, and political prisoners filled the jails. The people were tired and desperate. Everyone was worried. Something had to be done.

The meeting at Unity House was ostensibly to prepare for a national celebration. On June 30, dancing and singing were to fill the marketplaces and streets of villages all over the

D.D.R. What bands there were, were to strike up music; refreshment stands and shooting-galleries were to be set up; and the state theater groups were to offer their best programs. A national festival was in the making, more splendid and glorious than any held before. The name of the organization making these plans was the Commission for the Preparation of Comrade Walter Ulbricht's Sixtieth Birthday.

The Chairman of the Commission, Lotte Ulbricht, said that strict secrecy was to prevail in the preparations. Her husband, the General Secretary, was to be kept in the dark. But the unusually firm hand with which she ran things dispelled any doubts on the question: The General Secretary knew all about it. He had obviously "studied the general plan" behind the scenes and approved it.

The "general plan," or "basic concept," as they called it, sounded familiar to some of the functionaries. No one, including Mrs. Ulbricht, said it, but everyone knew from what source it derived: Stalin's seventieth birthday had been celebrated in December, 1949, with similar extravagance. Lotte Ulbricht spoke of an official state affair in the Friedrichstadpalast, of glittering receptions and testimonial banquets, of *Festschriften* honoring Ulbricht—*Walter Ulbricht: Fighter Against War and Fascism, Walter Ulbricht: Fighter for German Unity.* The Free Youth organization printed a million copies of a book on *Ulbricht and Youth,* bound in red imitation leather embossed with a picture of Ulbricht. Gifts, Mrs. Ulbricht said, were just as important as books: Beautiful, "distinctive" gifts had to come not only from all parts of East Germany, but from West Germany as well, so that after the birthday a great exhibition could be arranged.

On June 5, the new Soviet High Commissioner for Germany, Vladimir Semyonov, arrived in East Berlin. The next day, he invited German Party leaders to meet with him, and the conversation quickly turned to the birthday preparations. The High Commissioner said, "We'd like to advise Comrade Ulbricht to celebrate his sixtieth birthday in the same way Comrade Lenin celebrated his fiftieth." What had Lenin done? "Comrade Lenin invited a few guests in for the evening."

Ulbricht's birthday preparations were immediately called off. The books and testimonial volumes that had already been printed were pulped. There were difficult weeks ahead for Ulbricht; the "birthday order" was just one indication.* Much worse was the fact that new directives came from Moscow that knocked the bottom out of his policies. Semyonov handed the SED leaders a statement prepared in the Kremlin that was translated into German and published on June 11 as a Politburo resolution. With this resolution, later known as the "Declaration of the New Course," the "construction of Socialism in the D.D.R." ground to a halt.

Ulbricht had ordered the general campaign against private property at the Second SED Party Conference in July, 1952. In the following months, his functionaries were on the march —forcing farmers and artisans into "producer cooperatives," expropriating industrialists and businessmen, and arresting all those who resisted. Now the Declaration of the New Course suddenly ordered them to stop the expropriations and return the confiscated enterprises and collectivized farms to their original owners. Manufacturers and individual farmers were to receive credit from the state, and the people who had been

---

* The only reference to Ulbricht's sixtieth birthday in *Neues Deutschland* was a congratulatory message from the SED Central Committee, printed on Page 5. The Soviet leadership confined itself to a brief message in *Pravda*, which, contrary to custom, did not refer to Ulbricht as General Secretary but merely as one of the best-known organizers and leaders of the SED. (Leonhard, *The Kremlin Since Stalin* [New York: Frederick A. Praeger, 1962], pp. 71–72.)

jailed during the campaign were to be released. Banners and posters calling on the people to "build Socialism" or merely containing the word "Socialism" were to be "unobtrusively" withdrawn.

Party officials of the lower and middle levels were completely confused. It seemed as if their leaders were demanding that they undo today what they had been told to do yesterday. A Berlin district secretary expressed the feelings of the few *apparatchiks:* Never before had Moscow so agonizingly compromised the Party leadership. Semyonov had treated them like schoolchildren and simply read them the new lesson.

Ulbricht was compromised most of all, since he, as General Secretary and leading proponent of the "hard" line, was considered the originator of the discarded policy. He had announced it, identified himself with it, repeatedly defended it against attacks from the Party ranks. And Semyonov had directed his most savage criticism against Ulbricht at the Politburo sessions between June 6 and June 10. It appeared that after Stalin's death in March, Ulbricht had become *persona non grata* in Moscow.

Much had changed in East Berlin as well as in Moscow in the weeks following Stalin's death. What happened now was also unusual. Ulbricht, the man whom his enemies had called a "puppet," a "tool of the Kremlin," was resisting Moscow.

In late 1952 and early 1953, the effects of hasty socialization in East Germany had already precipitated differences among the German Communists. Ulbricht had sternly rejected proposals made in November, 1952, to increase investments in light industry in order to ease the plight of the people; he insisted that, under Socialism, heavy industry had priority. But three months later, Ulbricht could not ignore the signs that East Germany was heading for economic bankruptcy. By February, 1953, according to Grotewohl, most of the Politburo believed that a "quick change in the situation" was necessary but that it could not be effected without foreign aid. Ulbricht had counted on Stalin, who had ordered the forced socialization, to come to his aid with a powerful injection of rubles into the East German economy. After Stalin's death, he was forced to turn to the dictator's heirs. On April 15, Moscow not only told the German leaders to forget about economic aid but insisted that the SED change its policy. The "hard line," socialization, had to be discontinued.

But an astonishing thing happened: Ulbricht refused to comply with Moscow's order. He may have thought Stalin's heirs were at the point of betraying their legacy, but he probably knew or had reason to believe that a power struggle was being waged in the Kremlin. Though its outcome was in doubt, there was the possibility that the "conciliators" in Moscow—those who wanted Ulbricht to retreat—would be defeated by the "hard liners," men like Molotov. If people like Beria, or perhaps Malenkov, won, however, Ulbricht would not remain their agent in East Berlin. The German General Secretary therefore resisted the New Course not merely out of conviction, but for reasons of self-preservation as well. Still, his decision was astonishing. Stalin's death had released Ulbricht from the necessity of obedience, but he decided in favor of Stalin once again.

His most urgent task was still to solve the economic crisis. (This, of course, would strengthen his own position as General Secretary.) Ulbricht tried to do this in a manner that was precisely contrary to Moscow's advice: He tightened the screws instead of loosening them. In a speech to high Party leaders and government Ministers and Secretaries, the General Secretary vigorously endorsed the principles of Stalinist policy. He invoked that "wise teacher of Socialist construction, J. V. Stalin," demanded "greater vigilance . . . exposure of agents and diversionists . . . the dismissal of officials who merely talk and don't provide leadership," and explained away the current difficulties as the product of "sabotage, arson, and theft of documents." The most pressing problem, he said, was "to overcome the low work norms."[1] Six weeks later, on May 28, the government followed up a Central Committee resolution by decreeing an increase of at least 10 per cent in the work norms of state-owned factories.

The Kremlin was in no mood to accept this defiance of its wishes. On June 3, the Soviet Politburo made clear for a second time that it was watching developments in the D.D.R. with increasing skepticism and concern, and that a revision in policy was *urgently* required. Two days later, the Soviet High Commissioner appeared on the scene with the order for the New Course. But Ulbricht still did not give up. (There were indications of support for his views among members of the State Planning Commission.[2]) SED newspapers printed the Declaration of the New Course without comment on June 11. The General Secretary refused to lend his name to it, and he avoided taking a public position until the evening of June 16. He considered the policy of retreat basically wrong, and by his stubborn resistance, he wrested concessions from the other side.

Semyonov had obviously come to Berlin to explain the new order to the SED Central Committee, since it involved a 180° turn in policy. But Ulbricht had good reasons for not wanting to convene the Central Committee. In the factories and on construction sites, indignant workers were pressing Party and trade-union representatives to have the decree increasing the work norms rescinded, and the members of the Central Committee would certainly propose to do so at a plenary meeting. Yet the old work norms were too low, and

Semyonov knew it. It is probable that Semyonov yielded to Ulbricht on two points: not to make any changes in the new work norms, and not to convene the Central Committee.

This lifted a great weight from Ulbricht's mind, for there existed the danger that partisans of Dahlem, who had fallen into disgrace in May, if given the opportunity at a Central Committee meeting, might unite with the Politburo members who were trying to oust Ulbricht, to elect a new General Secretary. Since Semyonov's arrival, a rumor had spread in high Party circles that Ulbricht was on the way out. People in the Berlin district leadership, for example, were saying that the list for a completely new Politburo had already been drawn up; the Soviet authorities at Karlshorst had asked an important member of the State Planning Commission whether the population would welcome Ulbricht's resignation.[3] Two names always came up along with Ulbricht's in whispered conversations: Zaisser and Herrnstadt. The Minister for State Security and the Editor-in-Chief of *Neues Deutschland*, in other words, were leading the opposition to Ulbricht in the Politburo.

Zaisser and Herrnstadt had begun to look for allies in their struggle with Ulbricht even before June, 1953. They had been encouraged by Moscow's reply of April 15 to the SED Politburo and most certainly by friends and protectors in the Soviet capital. We have no detailed knowledge of their maneuverings, and it is not known whether they made their plans before Semyonov's arrival. The charges later brought against them seem to have preserved a deliberate silence on what really happened. But it is revealing that Hans Jendretzky, first Berlin district secretary, submitted his May Day speech to Herrnstadt for approval, not to Ulbricht. In it, he said nothing at all about Socialist construction but a great deal about Churchill's proposal for a Summit Conference.

He also discussed Premier Malenkov's statement that he welcomed every initiative to eliminate conflicts through negotiation. Herrnstadt changed nothing in the manuscript—except that he added a second name in those passages dealing with Malenkov's willingness to negotiate: Beria. For, while Ulbricht hoped that men like Molotov and Kaganovich would prevail in the struggle among Stalin's successors, Zaisser and Herrnstadt were betting on Malenkov and Beria. The conservatives invoked the spirit of the man under whose rule the Soviet Union had become a state stretching to the borders of Germany; the reformers were convinced that this great transcontinental expanse could not be pacified by force or terror, and they were trying to win an ally whom they, like their Party opponents, had disregarded until then: the people.

Zaisser and Herrnstadt evidently worked out a political platform during the first two weeks of June and distributed it to those officials whose support they hoped to win. (Ulbricht later indicated that they had submitted their proposals on policy and personnel to a Politburo subcommittee that "prepared organizational questions for the Central Committee's consideration." No further information on this subcommittee is available.) In it, they argued that the policies of the Party and government had been "basically wrong" and had fanned the flames of smoldering conflict, first evident immediately after the war, between the people and the "organs of power." A basic change of course required drastic changes in the SED and a new economic policy. But first a new Party leadership had to be installed.* Herrnstadt would

---

* Their proposals were never published in full either in the D.D.R. or in the West. But basic points can be deduced from Ulbricht's and Grotewohl's speeches at the Fifteenth Plenum of the SED Central Committee in July, 1953, and speeches by Hermann Matern, chairman of the Party's Central Control Commission.

replace Ulbricht as General Secretary and Zaisser would become Minister of Interior. We may conclude from this that both men were ready to accept Grotewohl as premier. On the other hand, Matern and Honecker were to be ousted from the Politburo together with Ulbricht, and the trade-union leadership was to be changed too. Simultaneously, Zaisser and Herrnstadt planned a purge of the "degenerated" Party apparatus "from top to bottom." As for their program of economic reform, all we know is that after their defeat, the victor said, "its realization would have led to a 'restoration of capitalism.'" We may assume that Zaisser and Herrnstadt considered greater concessions to the middle class necessary, and that they were even ready to refrain from collectivizing agriculture for a long time to come.

Through one of Dahlem's "blunders," as Ulbricht later called it, Hermann Matern got wind of the Zaisser-Herrnstadt platform and demanded that it be submitted to the Politburo. This took place on June 16, 1953, and the crisis in the Party leadership reached its climax. The rebels would now discover how many supporters they had in the SED's ruling circle.

Four of the Politburo's fourteen members and alternates were more or less openly committed to the anti-Ulbricht group, first and foremost among them Anton Ackermann, advocate until 1948 of a "German road to Socialism"— whom Herrnstadt considered a "dangerous deviationist"; Ackermann's former wife, Elli Schmidt, chairman of the Communist Women's League; Hans Jendretzky; and Deputy Premier Heinrich Rau. Only two, Matern and Honecker, supported Ulbricht outright. The others played a waiting game, watching to see who would win. According to off-the-record remarks made by Honecker, the majority sympathized with Zaisser and Herrnstadt.

As the two factions fought behind closed doors, an uninvited third group appeared on the scene: the workers. A representative of the Berlin Party leadership, Brandt by name, came to Unity House, where the Politburo was meeting, and asked to see Jendretzky. Jendretzky emerged with Herrnstadt, and Brandt reported to them that a column of protesting workers was marching down Stalinallee demanding that the increase in the work norms be rescinded. It had to be done right away. "You mean," Herrnstadt asked, "we must support the workers' demands—they are justified?" Brandt said that indeed they were. Both Party leaders said they would take the necessary steps and returned to the meeting.

Brandt sat down and waited. At one point, Semyonov came out to get some reports and went back in again. Several hours passed. Finally, Ulbricht appeared. The Politburo, he said, had reduced the work norms; Bruno Baum, the Berlin district secretary, was to tell the demonstrators and persuade them to disperse. The General Secretary could hardly conceal his agitation. But when Baum, accompanied by Brandt, reached the workers' procession at Alexanderplatz, the crowd had swelled to several thousand people, and more were coming in from the side streets. People waved to the demonstrators from the windows of apartment houses and government buildings. Slogans were being shouted: "We want to be free men, not slaves!" "We want free elections!" "Ulbricht must go!" "Goatee, belly, and glasses are not the will of the masses!" Baum gave up: "Nothing more can be done here."

Returning to Party headquarters, Baum learned that the East Berlin Chief of Police, Waldemar Schmidt, had moved against the growing crowds of demonstrators and wanted to arrest the "ringleaders" but that the Soviet military authorities had forbidden it. The Police Chief, swearing at the "weak-kneed Russians," proposed that Jendretzky be sent to persuade them to change their minds. But Jendretzky refused, saying he had no intention of slaughtering the demonstrators.

In the meantime, the crowd had reached the main government building. The leaders of the demonstration demanded to see Grotewohl and Ulbricht. One of the few people in the building who had not panicked—Selbmann, the Minister of Industry—phoned Ulbricht and pleaded with him to meet with the workers. Ulbricht replied that he was in a meeting and could not be disturbed. Again Selbmann pressed him, and Ulbricht replied: "It's raining, they'll probably disperse anyway."

A day earlier, Bruno Baum had already given a similar example of how the SED leaders felt. Grotewohl had sent a messenger to Berlin district headquarters with a letter he had received from Berlin construction workers demanding that the increase in work norms be abolished; they would send a delegation the next day for a reply, they said, and would strike if their demands were rejected. Baum instructed the messenger to tell Grotewohl not to yield under any circumstances. When the workers' delegation walked into the Premier's red-carpeted office on June 16, they would most certainly be awed by their surroundings and behave meekly. That was the capitalist heritage.

On the evening of June 16, Ulbricht and Grotewohl addressed a hastily summoned meeting of selected Party activists and announced that the increase in norms had been rescinded. For the first time, Ulbricht publicly endorsed the New Course and said, "The Party is abandoning an admittedly mistaken road and taking the right one."[4] But it was too late.

By the next morning, June 17, the workers' uprising of East Berlin had spread to all parts of East Germany. During the morning, Ulbricht left Unity House (probably in a Soviet tank) and withdrew to a farm belonging to the Central Committee in Kienbaum, near a Soviet airfield. At noon, Soviet General Dibrova proclaimed a state of emergency. The occupation forces took command, established martial law, sent out tank patrols, and ordered the troops to fire on demonstrators who refused to obey orders to disperse. Military tribunals were set up, death sentences were handed down and carried out on the spot. By evening, the revolt in Berlin had been crushed. Ulbricht returned.

The Politburo met again. For it was of the utmost importance to prepare a report for Moscow—far more urgent than the resolution of differences among the Party leaders. The Kremlin was waiting to be told how the events of June 16 and 17 had ever come to pass. It is not known how the SED leaders excused themselves in this report, but on June 23, SED newspapers published the public version of the uprising. And, two days earlier, the Central Committee had approved a Politburo declaration labeling it a "fascist provocation":

The enemy . . . picked Tuesday, June 16, for the start of the provocation. He hurled his gangster columns, armed with guns and oil-filled bottles, across the sector border. Their job was to get the construction workers to lay down their tools and to mislead them with inflammatory slogans into a demonstration against the government. Arson, looting, and shooting were to give the demonstration the appearance of an uprising. The enemy instructed its agents to organize similar actions in other parts of the Republic . . . on the following day. The fascist scum who had sneaked over from West Berlin and who were directed from there, organized attacks on food warehouses, school dormitories, clubhouses, and shops, as well as attempts on the lives of functionaries. . . . That was how a fascist regime was to be established in the D.D.R. and Germany's road to unity and peace destroyed.[5]

The uprising, it continued, had been instigated by American and German warmongers who were panic-stricken by the successes of the Socialist camp and the New Course, but the majority of the population, especially the workers, had energetically repulsed the provocateurs.

The members of the Central Committee may have wondered why the report and summary presented at this important meeting were given not by Ulbricht but by Grotewohl, who also chaired the session. Did Ulbricht want thereby to shift responsibility to the Premier for what was being said in the Party's name about the uprising? Or was it perhaps that the Soviets did not want Ulbricht to preside? This second possibility seemed more probable, since the Russians must have asked themselves whether the most hated man in Germany was still of use to them. Had the revolt improved Zaisser's and Herrnstadt's chances?

Naturally, each of the two groups in the Politburo tried to blame the other for what had happened. Zaisser and Herrnstadt could rightfully say the uprising had been caused by Ulbricht's erroneous policies, which had had adverse effects on all parts of the population. And the General Secretary himself was not without a defense: Had not the increase in work norms caused the revolt? But neither the Russians nor Zaisser and Herrnstadt had objected to it. True, Herrnstadt had published articles in *Neues Deutschland* between June 11 and June 16 condemning the methods of officials in charge of maintaining the work norms, but he had not challenged the decree itself. These articles, Ulbricht now said, had spurred the dissatisfied elements in the population on to violence. As for the norms, all the Party leaders were in the same boat, for no one of them had suspected the effects the directive would produce, and everyone had agreed to it.

Ulbricht had his own view on the causes of the uprising.

His opponents felt they had been proved right, and he felt that he had. Though he had to state the opposite publicly, no one could shake his belief that the New Course, the policy of slacking the reins, of "retreat," of openly admitting weaknesses and difficulties, had ignited the explosion. There would have been no such outbreaks under Stalin. Were not those who now demanded Ulbricht's head the spokesmen for prisoners awaiting final sentence, spokesmen for "fascist ringleaders"?

The power struggle in the Politburo had already been decided in Ulbricht's favor when Central Committee members, to their surprise, were recalled to Berlin during the last week in July. (The Central Committee had only rarely convened during the preceding three years.) Ulbricht and Grotewohl reported to the Plenum on the recent disputes, and now accused Zaisser and Herrnstadt publicly of having formed an "anti-Party faction with a defeatist line aimed at destroying the Party's unity." Their platform was the main evidence supposedly substantiating this charge, but it was not submitted for discussion; the Central Committee's only task was to concur in the sentence already passed. The judgment would not be official until Moscow had approved it.

Why had the Soviet Union abandoned Zaisser and Herrnstadt? The answer is simple: Zaisser and Herrnstadt had backed the wrong man: Beria. On July 9, the Kremlin announced that Beria had been stripped of all his responsibilities and arrested "as an enemy of the Party and State." A letter from Moscow, described by Grotewohl as the "Beria document," was now read to the members of the Central Committee, in which the long-time Soviet Minister of the Interior was accused of "many" crimes and of following a "policy of capitulation" whose inevitable outcome was the restoration of capitalism. His willingness to compromise on German policy, it was charged, could have led to the downfall of the D.D.R. Ulbricht's and Grotewohl's accusations against Beria's German supporters sounded the same note. Like Beria, the East German Minister of State Security was also charged with having tried to free his ministry from Party control in order to create an independent instrument of power. And Zaisser was also linked to Beria in Ulbricht's accusation that he had held discussions with special representatives from Beria without informing the Politburo. Indeed, the German Party leaders tried as hard as they could to convict Zaisser and Herrnstadt of being Beria's co-conspirators, but they lacked the evidence to make this serious accusation stick. (At the Fourth SED Party Congress, in March–April, 1954, Hermann Matern had to confess that there was no proof "of the criminal Beria's direct influence," although, said Matern, "it had guided Zaisser's and Herrnstadt's activities." "The facts disclosed in Beria's trial fit into their anti-Party factional activity."[6]) Nevertheless, by the end of July, Zaisser and Herrnstadt were dismissed from their posts and lost their places in the Party leadership. In January, 1954, they were expelled from the SED, a month after Beria was sentenced to death. This sequence of events emphasized once more the link between the two cases. If what was said and written in Moscow and Berlin during 1953 (and later) about the ideas of these three men is true, then there is no denying that their intentions coincided: to ease domestic tensions by concessions to all parts of the population; to ease international tensions by concessions to the Western powers. Germany was the laboratory where these policies were to be tested, policies the other Party leaders considered reckless and dangerous—especially after the June uprising.

And this is the tragedy of June 17: The workers' revolt did not overthrow Ulbricht—it saved him. His ouster was one of the workers' major demands, but after initial wavering, the Kremlin decided that surrender to this demand would involve great loss of face and might be interpreted as a concession made from weakness, leading in turn to new disturbances with even more far-reaching demands. The Soviet leaders imposed certain conditions together with their decision, of course: Ulbricht was to engage in "self-criticism" of his previous conduct and he was to support the New Course wholeheartedly.

Ulbricht was in no position to continue his resistance to the New Course after what had happened in the preceding weeks. He had learned only too well—from the revolt and from the fate of Beria—what was at stake. He humbled himself and confessed to the Central Committee: "I would like to say openly before the highest forum of the Party that among Party leaders I bear the greatest responsibility for . . . the errors that have been committed."[7]

Ulbricht also admitted that he had ignored the "principle of collective leadership" (proclaimed after Stalin's death) by making individual decisions, and that he had "subordinated the Politburo to the Secretariat." Not only did Zaisser, Herrnstadt, and their supporters—Ackermann, Jendretzky, and Elli Schmidt—lose their Party posts, therefore, but some of Ulbricht's followers as well. The Secretariat, so important to Ulbricht's power in the Party, was reduced from eleven to six members. Ulbricht's title was changed from General Secretary to First Secretary of the Central Committee. This was more than an imitation of Soviet practices; his new title was meant to symbolize his position as *primus inter pares.*

Ulbricht now openly avowed the New Course, and a new Central Committee resolution reaffirmed its essential aim: "to improve the economic and political situation in the German Democratic Republic, and on this basis, significantly to raise the living standard of the working class and all other toilers in the Republic."[8] The production of consumer goods was to be expanded with financial help from the Soviet Union.[9] Ulbricht and other Party leaders also promised to inject life into the five-party bloc, the People's Chamber and other formal representative bodies; legal rights were to be guaranteed, sentences for political crimes reduced, and certain groups of prisoners amnestied. Relationships between church and state were to be normalized, and scientists and artists were promised "the possibility of working creatively." Two months later, Ulbricht called for more tolerance toward democratic-bourgeois literature and popular amusements.[10] The government-controlled film company (DEFA) was to produce romantic movies; cabarets were to have greater freedom of expression; and nonpolitical magazines were to be published again. Cultural life lost some of its monotony. "The New Course," said Ulbricht in the summer of 1954, replying to alleged queries from citizens, "will prevail during the entire period of struggle for the national reunification of Germany."[11]

Twelve months later, however, Ulbricht was saying something quite different to the members of the Central Committee:

Some of you will wonder why I haven't used the phrase "New Course." . . . It has given a lot of people strange ideas—namely, that it is possible to consume more than is produced, that wages can rise faster than productivity . . . that it is all right to loaf on the job. . . . The ideological effects have been just as obvious. Neutrality toward bourgeois ideology and superstition has grown. Our call to foster a happy life for the working masses has led many functionaries to encourage a selfish, materialistic outlook. What is more remarkable about this Course is not that it is new, but that it is wrong. I must warn people with these ideas that we never meant to, and never will, embark on this kind of mistaken course.[12]

Ulbricht's opportunism in the summer of 1953 had paid off. Malenkov, initiator of the New Course in the Soviet Union, had been dismissed as Chairman of the Council of Ministers in February, 1955. Ulbricht's crises seemed at an end.

The High Art of Tactics

An event beyond Ulbricht's control had precipitated the first serious crisis of his career: Stalin's death. But even after this crisis had been resolved, Ulbricht's fate was bound up with Stalin's name, and the denunciation of Stalin brought a second crisis into Ulbricht's life.

The Twentieth Congress of the Communist Party of the Soviet Union was held in Moscow from February 14 to 26, 1956. Communists and anti-Communists alike were stunned when the speakers, led by Khrushchev and Mikoyan, accused the idol Stalin, the infallible teacher of Marxism-Leninism and leader of world Communism, of countless terrorist acts and charged him with personal responsibility for the purges of 1936–38. A number of formerly prominent Party leaders, arrested and imprisoned by Stalin as traitors and as enemies of the people, were rehabilitated. The Bolshevik catechism, the *History of the Communist Party of the Soviet Union,* written under Stalin's orders, was labelled a series of falsifications; it had helped foster Stalin's cult of personality, it was said, and was to be discarded as a textbook.

At the Congress, the new CPSU leaders also announced another decision that was destined to have even greater political effect than the shattering of the Stalin myth *per se:* Certain Bolshevik principles that had been treated as dogma in the Stalinist era were now to be revised. Wars, said Khrushchev, contradicting Stalin, could be prevented. There were also different roads to the achievement of Socialism, and the parliamentary road to Socialist power—which did not require the exercise of revolutionary force—could no longer be ignored. Finally, the class struggle did not, as Stalin had maintained, intensify as Socialist construction advanced, but rather weakened. In repudiating the Stalinist dogmas, the new Soviet rulers voiced their hope of reconciling all layers of the population in the Soviet world; henceforth, voluntary cooperation by the masses was to take the place of bureau-cratic rule and coercive government action.

In part, the decisions revealed at the Twentieth Congress did little more than codify changes that had already occurred in Soviet life. But taken in their totality, they initiated a new period in Bolshevik policy. The West watched and waited attentively; the Communist parties in Eastern and Western Europe felt impelled to draw conclusions from the Moscow Congress.

Ulbricht was not ready to welcome an open admission of guilt and crime or a departure from the principles of Stalinist rule. He was one of a number of East European functionaries who had misgivings about the Twentieth Congress, fearing it would force the Communist parties into a "discussion of errors" and put them on the defensive. But Ulbricht had learned from the past. He had no intention of repeating his most serious mistake—open resistance to Moscow. On the contrary, he decided to accede immediately to the "new line," pay the necessary tribute to the Kremlin, but then skillfully, intelligently, and cautiously block de-Stalinization in the D.D.R. as well as he could.

Taking his cues from Khrushchev's famous, and still secret, speech at the Twentieth Congress, Ulbricht began to polemicize furiously against Stalin and those who believed in him. He did not report the source of his new inspirations. "The young comrades," Ulbricht now said, "are by and large educated so that they know certain dogmas by heart. They know more about Stalin's biography than the entire Politburo does. They can quote dates and anything else you can think of from memory. But if you ask them what's our point of view on questions of Socialist economics, they don't know."[13] (In the past, Ulbricht had considered "the study of Comrade Stalin's work and life were of particular importance."[14]) Stalin did not adequately prepare the Soviet Union for World War II, Ulbricht continued, and ignored the opinions of his military advisers. (Four years before, Ulbricht had said that Stalin's strategic genius had had great influence on the course of World War II and called him a "military genius.")

Ulbricht's remarks about Stalin's importance were greeted with great indignation. The German Communists had not forgotten that Ulbricht had considered Stalin "one of the greatest living theoreticians of scientific Socialism," the "greatest scientist of the present epoch, whose life's work would affect history for centuries to come." Now he was suddenly saying, "We have never denied that Stalin was a Marxist, even an outstanding Marxist," but "we cannot count Stalin among the Marxist classics." But these criticisms of Stalin were not followed by deed. In order to prevent any such action, Ulbricht decided to make his 1953 defeat appear as a triumph.

After Stalin's death, Soviet leaders had attacked Ulbricht for ignoring the "special conditions in Germany" and "underestimating the national question"—in other words, for slavishly copying the Soviet Union.* They had forced him to make some political modifications and had tried to check his

---

* Grotewohl, for example, at the fifteenth plenary meeting of the Central Committee, in July, 1953, said, "In the last two years . . . we made . . . the error of not altogether correctly appraising the international situation and, along with it, the national problem in Germany. . . . We underestimated the national question." (*Das 15. Plenum des Zentralkomitees der SED—Parteinternes Material.*)

autocratic rule. Now, Ulbricht set out to exploit this. For if it was wrong slavishly to follow Soviet policy in 1953, it was equally wrong in 1956. Due weight must still be given to the "special conditions in Germany." And in 1953, had not the New Course and collective leadership been introduced more quickly and consistently in East Germany—albeit against Ulbricht's will—than in the other people's democracies? Ulbricht went further. He remembered that in 1945, the Soviets had ordered Ackermann to work out the thesis of a "peaceful, democratic road to Socialism." It had been scrapped in 1948– 49, but now it could be exploited again. Soon Ulbricht was arguing that the East German Communist Party had been pursuing the "peaceful, democratic road to Socialism" since 1945, although he had to admit that "many people did not know it."[15] Pursuing this line of thought a step further, one could argue that if Stalinism had never existed in East Germany, there was no need for de-Stalinization. The disastrous cult of personality had never flourished there as it had in the Soviet Union and the other people's democracies. As to the question of how such a different policy had been possible at the time, Ulbricht had an astonishing answer: The Soviet occupation authorities, he said, had been Leninists.

Ulbricht was undoubtedly aware that when a people have been thrown off balance—and there were more than enough reasons for that in the SED—one can hardly set them straight with mere words. He decided, therefore, to turn the attention of the confused Party officers and members to a "new" task, economic policy, as a means of making them forget their confusion.

In other East European countries, hated officials were being dismissed from their posts, and stormy discussions were raging over what should be done in light of the Twentieth Party Congress. But at the SED Party Conference in March, 1956,

Ulbricht concentrated on the D.D.R.'s Second Five Year Plan and did not once mention Stalin's name—in a speech that ran to 200 pages. In April, he told a meeting of Leipzig Party workers that the main task was "to attain absolute superiority over the . . . capitalist countries" and repeatedly emphasized "absolute superiority." In July, he explained to the Central Committee that "the question of the cult of personality" had in no sense been the major topic at the Twentieth Congress; economic policy had played an incomparably greater role. "There is now no more important problem," Ulbricht said, "than the struggle to increase labor productivity and reduce costs." Those who wanted to keep harping on "the question of the cult of personality" were influenced by counterrevolutionary forces and in turn supported them.[16]

Ulbricht was aware of Khrushchev's wish to meet the needs of the Soviet bloc economies and prove "Socialism's superiority over capitalism in the economic race," and he surely knew that the D.D.R. had a special part to play in this competition: It was and is the second strongest industrial power in the Soviet world, and it had the inevitable but particularly difficult problem of having to catch up with and surpass the Federal Republic. Ulbricht could tell the SED members to "think less about the past and more about the economy" without fearing Moscow's wrath. The Soviet Union approved of his economic program, as its large grant of rubles in the summer of 1956 proved.

In the months following the Twentieth Party Congress, Ulbricht tried as skillfully as he knew how to suppress the new and, for him, distasteful and dangerous "discussion of errors." It was imperative for him to minimize the importance of the Congress to both international and German Communism. Not only did his attempts to smooth things over fail, but they multiplied his troubles.

Immediately after the Twentieth Congress, it was quite apparent that confusion and uncertainty beset the officials at Unity House. Once the Party workers recovered from their initial shock, however, they began to press for a full discussion of the import of the Twentieth Congress. Party officials were overwhelmed with questions: Why are the Communist parties only now being told of Stalin's many errors? Why did Stalin's closest collaborators not protest against his decisions during his lifetime? What arguments can be used to convince the people of the correct new attitude toward Stalin without destroying the Party's prestige? Why was Khrushchev's secret speech, which we hear about on the Western radio, not published in the SED press? Are the people who were unjustly imprisoned during the Stalin era in the D.D.R. going to be rehabilitated? Why have no Ministers of the D.D.R. been ousted? Why are those who used Stalin-like methods in the D.D.R. not called to account?

Some of the questioning East Germans, particularly the Party intellectuals, had expected the whole matter of how to carry out de-Stalinization to be discussed and decided upon at the Party Conference set for March, but they were disappointed. When Ulbricht reported on the Five Year Plan, the cultivation of corn in the D.D.R., and "the growing economic crisis in the Federal Republic," several dozen delegates left the meeting to express their indignation outside and to exchange ideas on how to force a real discussion of the Twentieth Congress. They considered taking the floor to protest the manner in which the meeting was being railroaded, but this was actually impossible, since anyone wanting to take part in the debate had to submit a copy of his remarks beforehand and, if he made the slightest departure from the approved text, he would be cut down.

The official conference proceeded, therefore, exactly as the

First Secretary had planned it. Unofficially, however, the opinion grew that Ulbricht's dismissal was the most important consequence to be drawn from the decisions made at the CPSU Congress. Ulbricht had violated the "principle of collective leadership" by his dictatorial attitude and actions; he had been Stalin's willing tool in Germany; he was hated by the people and had discredited the Party. Furthermore, he was proving his incorrigible "Stalinism" again by his provocative reaction to the Twentieth Congress—condemning those who were not as quick as he to adopt the new jargon, while simultaneously blocking the new policies.

During the summer of 1956, the poet Bertolt Brecht called an informal meeting of writers and intellectuals. He told them that Ulbricht was an orthodox dictator who was alienated from the people, whose policies had completely destroyed the humanistic content of Socialism and had created an intolerable situation in the D.D.R. His friends agreed, but doubted that there were any capable German Communist leaders to replace him. Brecht remarked that offhand he could name fifteen men who could do a better job, and besides, he himself would prefer anyone to Ulbricht. (In other, similar conversations, Dahlem was frequently mentioned as Ulbricht's successor.) Throughout the summer, the rumors continued that Ulbricht's ouster was imminent.

The controversies over the Twentieth Congress soon reached the Politburo, where it was a constant topic of discussion at the regular Tuesday meetings. Ulbricht's deputy, Karl Schirdewan, whom Ulbricht had brought into the Politburo and Secretariat as Dahlem's successor in 1953, thought that the Party had not yet drawn the "proper conclusions" from the Soviet Party Congress. At a meeting of Central Committee functionaries, he said it was time to stop labeling those with differing viewpoints as enemies and deviationists. He and a few other high Party officials, among them Zaisser's successor as Minister for State Security, Ernst Wollweber, again criticized Ulbricht's despotic methods and his alienation from people and even from his closest colleagues. Ulbricht's response to these charges was that they represented "a surrender to hostile agitation" organized to topple him and ultimately the SED itself. In taking this line, Ulbricht could rely on the fact that disciplined Communists like Schirdewan and Wollweber would not dare, any more than Zaisser and Herrnstadt, to express their views directly to Party members or the public. They aired their grievances in closed meetings or among friends. Still, opposition to him within the Party was growing, and in the universities, the cry for intellectual freedom was becoming louder; Ulbricht was booed into silence while addressing a meeting at the Agricultural College in Leipzig. The Party leaders who opposed him were men he had trusted, and the new opposition did not appear to be influenced by the "class enemy," but rather was based on the policies of other Communists: Observing the Poles and Hungarians with sympathy and enthusiasm, they asked with increasing urgency why it was not possible for the D.D.R. to follow the same road.

In Poland, the security police were being purged, unjustly imprisoned people were being released and rehabilitated, about 36,000 persons, mostly political prisoners, had been amnestied, and especially hated Stalinists were being ousted from their jobs. Moreover, Polish Communists were able to go beyond a condemnation of Stalin and view their whole system critically. German Communists were particularly impressed with the fact that the Polish Communist Party leadership had in principle met the demands of the Posnan workers who had gone on strike in June, 1956. These events only confirmed the SED Party workers and intellectuals in their opposition to Ulbricht and strengthened their resistance to the man; he could obviously no longer read the signs of the time.

Ulbricht's speeches of the summer of 1956 reveal, however, that he had at least decided to meet the opposition half way. He admitted that questions and answers in the report on the Twentieth Congress had been "too simply" formulated; that the necessary conclusions had not yet been "analyzed in all their implications" at the Third SED Party Conference; and that his own statements had created "misunderstandings."[17] It was clear that for Ulbricht as well as for his opposition, a great deal now depended on the course of events in Poland and Hungary, on whether the progressive Communists there would succeed in their de-Stalinization. Ulbricht thought that the Hungarian comrades ought to take energetic measures against the "hostile discussions" in the Petofi Circle—a discussion group of Hungarian intellectuals, most of them from the Hungarian Youth Group, which became a sounding-board for political opposition to the Hungary Stalinist leadership— and that the dismissal of Rakosi, chairman of the Hungarian Communist Party, was an irreparable mistake. In a conversation with a high Hungarian official, he said, "Just keep on going the way you are. First you depose Rakosi, then you institute reforms, and the end result is collapse."

But at first, Ulbricht's foes appeared to be gaining ground. In Poland, on October 20, the former Party leader, Wladyslaw Gomulka, who had been released from prison a few months earlier, was again elected to his post in defiance of the Soviet Union. The national Communist program he announced and its internal political reforms went far beyond the Yugoslav model.

Since Ulbricht knew the effect that news of these proposed reforms would have on the Party opposition, he instructed the SED press to publish as little as possible on events in Warsaw and not to print the text of Gomulka's programmatic speech. Party workers were ordered to reject the "Gomulka propaganda of Polish comrades" as impermissible "interference in the affairs of another Party" and to prohibit visits by Polish delegations. But SED journalists printed Gomulka's speech secretly: The opposition now had one goal—a Polish October in the D.D.R.

With one stroke, however, everything changed. On October 23, revolution erupted in Hungary. Ulbricht must have realized that victory was near for him, despite any fears that the revolutionary wave might spill over into his own domain. Here was proof of how correct his tactic of delay and resistance had been; for the first time since June 17, 1953, here was proof of what danger lay ahead when a totalitarian regime loosened the reins. The opportunity had arrived to demonstrate to the Soviets and to his opponents "how to do things right." And in the last weeks of 1956, Ulbricht really did demonstrate what he had learned from Lenin and Stalin and in thirty years of work in the *apparat*. Hard on the heels of the Budapest revolution, Ulbricht ordered sweeping security arrangements throughout the D.D.R. In the factories, the SED Workers' Defense Groups, created after June 17, 1953, were activated and armed; field exercises were held; operational plans drawn up; and the army received emergency orders to be on the alert. "Hungary teaches," Ulbricht told Parliament on November 3, "that whoever gives even his little finger to reaction will end by losing his life."

Scanty, dishonest reports in the SED newspapers of events in East Europe continued, however, to arouse anger among the people and in the Party. SED workers besieged the Party leaders with requests to release Gomulka's speech. Ulbricht refused; the press "was not a seismograph to record mistaken ideas or anti-Marxist theories."[18] He was asked to permit the publication of more exact information on the Hungarian

revolution; this was "freedom for the propaganda of capitalist interests." None of the requests were granted.

But the unrest of the population, especially among the
students, could not be suppressed. Ulbricht prevailed upon
the other Politburo members to agree to additional measures:
the prohibition of all demonstrations; the arrest of all "ringleaders," "dissatisfied," and "opposition" elements; the organization of long "debates" behind closed doors. Threaten
the obstinate ones, and if you must, beat them up! Try by
every means to divide the opposition and drive a wedge between the intelligentsia and the rest of the population. Do not
provoke the workers, but try to incite their anger against the
students and other intellectuals! Exploit all antagonisms between the two groups! Ulbricht's orders were carried out.

When State Security Minister Wollweber informed top
Party leaders, during a parliamentary meeting on November
2, that "all hell had broken loose" in the Leuna Works and
that the plant managers feared that disturbances and "counterrevolutionary activity" would continue, confusion and inde-
cision spread among the bureaucrats. Grotewohl suggested
that one of them go to the plant and talk with the workers.
There were no volunteers. Grotewohl thought Fritz Selbmann,
Minister of Industry, ought to go, but Selbmann protested
vehemently: "I'll do nothing of the kind!" he said. "What
could I tell these people? If anyone goes, it should be Bruno
Leuschner [Chairman of the State Planning Commission]."
"But I have nothing to do with factories," Leuschner parried.
"The Ministries are responsible for factories. Either Selbmann or Winkler [Minister for Chemical Industries] should
go." Gerhard Ziller, Party Secretary for Economic Affairs,
was also named; Leuschner remarked that he had as much
jurisdiction as any of the others. The quarrel began to border
on the absurd.

Ulbricht had said nothing until then. His cold, small eyes peered into empty space. His cheek muscles were taut, and his lips pressed tight together. But then he laid down the law. "I don't understand your arguments. . . . Some gentlemen who are very close to the I.G.-Farben Trust have felt a hopeful breeze in Leuna, and they want to exploit our present difficulties in order to peddle I.G.-Farben ideology. Neither Leuschner, Selbmann, nor Ziller have anything to do with this. Erich Mielke (State Secretary in the Ministry for State Security) has to straighten things out. The four or five I.G.-Farben agents there must be uncovered; there aren't more than that. Once they're caught, Leuna will settled down, because agents in the other plants will learn about it. Then the Plan will be all right, our economic policy will be all right, everything in Leuna and the rest of the country will be all right. Isn't that true? I think, therefore, that Mielke ought to leave right now. Then we'll see what happens." (Mielke found the "agents.")[19]

The mood in the universities was also cause for alarm, particularly in the Humboldt University in Berlin and Leipzig's Karl Marx University. There and elsewhere, the students had assembled and, like their counterparts in Poland and Hungary, demanded sweeping educational reforms, the right to form their own organizations, official recognition of student delegations that did not have representatives of the government youth organization, and an end to the compulsory courses on Marxism-Leninism and the Russian language—in short, an education free of political control. Many of the students were convinced that demonstrations were necessary to back up their demands. Ulbricht immediately sent a number of high Party functionaries to keep the excited students from carrying out their plans, and to sap their energy by long speeches and engaging them in even longer discussions. But Ulbricht did not rely merely on persuasion; he also ordered the State

Security police to arrest some of the "ringleaders" as "agents" who were "taking orders from West Berlin." Army officers therefore accompanied the functionaries to make visible the power of the Workers' and Peasants' State. The university lecture halls, cabarets, and other places frequented by intellectuals were visited by strong-arm squads disguised as workers' delegations, who demanded political obedience "in the name of the toiling masses." Heeding Ulbricht's slogan, "The intellectuals need a good kick in the groin," they went into action with fists and clubs like the old Red Veterans' League.

Alfred Neumann, Berlin district secretary, reported to Ulbricht on what had happened to the "hotheads" at Humboldt University: "Just what you predicted. They held out for about two days, but after that, they were so worn out they went quietly off to bed. We had to get down to brass tacks with only three or four unreasonable fellows. Then everything was peaceful." Smiling, Ulbricht answered, "It's a completely democratic method. . . . I believe now we and the students know where we stand."

Opposition to Ulbricht in the universities—to the degree that it was not limited to small circles but embraced larger groups—was primarily concentrated in the medical and scientific schools, where many of the students were relatively apolitical. Had the future doctors, chemists, biologists, and physicists of East Germany been polled on their political views, a number of them—like their West German peers—would certainly have answered, "We simply want to pursue our studies." Others would perhaps have spoken of freedom and democracy, and of the Federal Republic as a model. For, despite ten years of Communist education, most of the students would still (or once again) have voiced "bourgeois ideas." There was little prospect of realizing them: The Communists had few doubts that the Soviet Union would rush to their aid against a "bourgeois opposition" imperiling the Workers' and Peasants' State. Socialist opposition, though smaller, was more dangerous. It alone could offer an alternate Socialist program that the Soviets might accept if they thought it advisable, or—bearing Poland in mind—necessary.

From Ulbricht's point of view, these opposition elements, particularly in the Party leadership, had to be shown how futile their efforts were, or at least, to what end their ideas might lead. At the very least, they had to be deterred and shown who had the power.

On December 1, 1956, the front page of *Neues Deutschland* reported that Dr. Wolfgang Harich (Professor of Philosophy at Humboldt University), Bernhard Steinberger, Manfred Hertwig, and Irene Giersch had been arrested two days earlier. The Harich group, it said, had tried to "undermine and destroy constitutional order in the German Democratic Republic. . . . The political goal of this anti-State group was capitalist restoration in the D.D.R." On March 9, 1957, the Supreme Court of the D.D.R. sentenced the first three to prison terms of ten, four, and two years, respectively. An example had been set.

Harich and his supporters, none of whom had the slightest desire to restore capitalism but wanted only to breathe new life into East German Communism, had drafted a reform program that rather faithfully reflected the ideas of the existing Socialist opposition to Ulbricht. This SED opposition, composed primarily of intellectuals, was unmistakably inspired by the Polish (not the Hungarian) model of an anti-Stalinist "revolution from above." Its goal was a reformed Communism free of Soviet domination and of Stalinism, adapted to specific German conditions so as to open up new possibilities for German reunification. More than a year later, events were to prove that these and similar hopes were not confined to the Harich circle.

Ulbricht had no scruples about using all the terrorist measures at his command in this period of crisis, but he also employed a carrot-and-stick policy, even granting dissident students some concessions. His greatest concern, however, lay with the workers, who had rebelled against him and the SED State while the intelligentsia had stood aside and waited. Now, with the intelligentsia in revolt, how would the workers react? Ulbricht wanted above all to prevent the kind of alliance that had been sealed between the two great opposition groups in Poland and Hungary. In this, he succeeded.

Ulbricht made as many concessions as he could to the workers during the winter months of 1956–57. The problem of work norms seemed to have disappeared: The parliament had passed a law raising old-age pensions even though the necessary funds were not available; it was announced that housing construction was being expanded and the 45-hour work week introduced. In the middle of November, Ulbricht promised that Workers' Committees would be established in the factories—a promise he retracted once the crisis had passed. (These proposed workers' committees were distinguished in more than name from the workers' councils in Yugoslavia and the newly established ones in Poland. They were not to have any power of decision over the plan and rate of production in their factories, but merely "take a position"; profit-sharing by the plant work force was also forbidden.)

The hoped-for effect of these concessions—a reconciliation between the regime and the working class—did not materialize, however. One goal was attained, though: The workers at least showed no solidarity with the rebellious intelligentsia. To begin with, the shock of their 1953 defeat was still strong. Then, they had hoped the West would come to their aid; now once more they saw in Hungary how an uprising was being put down by Soviet bullets and tanks. Was there any point in rebelling again? Many workers were completely ignorant of what was going on in the universities and among Party intellectuals. Moreover, Ulbricht and other SED leaders knew how skillfully to exploit their resentment of the intellectuals— particularly the "technical intelligentsia" (engineers, economists, chemists, etc.) who had been economically favored by the regime and, so the workers believed, thus corrupted. In any case, German intellectuals had never played the political role assumed by the Polish or Russian intelligentsia; they had never been recognized as spokesmen for workers' rights and progress. Justifiably or not, the workers did not trust them.

Ulbricht had won a round. He had made sure that the Polish example was not followed, and he had prevented the Hungarian revolution from spilling over into East Germany. His stock rose in Moscow. But almost a year passed before Khrushchev agreed to his eliminating a new anti-Ulbricht opposition, which had pinned its greatest hopes on the Kremlin.

On the morning of February 7, 1958, readers of *Neues Deutschland* were astonished to read on its front page that "the Plenum [of the Central Committee] was forced to deal with the activity of an opportunistic group that had tried to change the Party's political line." The next day, *Neues Deutschland* reported that "this opportunistic group had sat in the supreme councils of the Party." A Central Committee resolution on "Assignments of Posts in the Party Leadership" revealed that Politburo members Schirdewan and Oelssner, together with Minister of State Security Wollweber, had lost their Party positions.

In 1956, Schirdewan had been assigned to prepare the Politburo report for the plenary meeting of the Central Com-

mittee in November. His draft had been sharply criticized at
two Politburo sessions because, according to Ulbricht, it contained two "basic errors: . . . an underestimation of NATO
policy and of the ambitious attempts of the German militarists
to undermine the German Democratic Republic; it talked of
democratization, but not of the need for security measures to
check the enemy's subversive activity." Ulbricht had demanded
that a reference to the activity of hostile groups and an appeal
for vigilance be added. But Schirdewan was not to be deferred;
he drew comparisons between the situation in the D.D.R. and
Hungary, and tried to block coercive measures against defiant
students and intellectuals. He believed "ideological persuasion
would do the job" and that the "safety-valve tactic" had to be
used. When Ulbricht continued strongly to oppose him, he
attacked in turn and, as Honecker said later, "went over to
unprincipled struggle." The roots of his attitude, Honecker
went on to say, "unquestionably lie in the misinterpretation
of the Twentieth Congress decision by Comrade Schirdewan
and others." "The others" meant Wollweber, first of all. He,
too, had "incorrectly estimated the situation" in 1956, had
"criminally neglected the struggle against enemy agents,"
and had prevented the State Security police from "performing
their duties properly."

When the time arrived to settle accounts, Schirdewan and
Wollweber were accused, as Zaisser and Herrnstadt had been
five years earlier, of being an active anti-Party faction. Since
two people hardly constitute a faction, other "faction" members had to be found: Fred Oelssner, then head of the Committee on Problems of Consumer Goods Production and Food
Supplies and presently Director of the Institute of Economic
Science of the Academy of Science; Gerhard Ziller, who
killed himself in December, 1957; and Fritz Selbmann, Deputy Premier. The "technicians" agreed with the "politicians"

on two points: They, too, wanted to oust Ulbricht from leadership because they thought him incompetent and his policies wrong, and they considered that Ulbricht ignored the special conditions of the divided country, especially since he had again insisted in 1957 that policy and propaganda emphasize the unity of the regimes and Communist parties of the Socialist camp, not the unique qualities of each country within it.

A later "indictment" declared that Schirdewan had not seen the dangers in the "illusory idea" of "German unity at any price"; that Oelssner was an "opportunist" in agricultural policy who wanted to dissolve unprofitable collective farms and who, with Selbmann, considered it absurd to imitate the structural changes being made in the Soviet economy, as Ulbricht had ordered in 1957. Selbmann was reported to have said: "What they're doing in the Soviet Union now is out of the question for us."

Ulbricht warned his enemies several times before crushing them. The Harich trials in March and July, 1957, were the first occasion. But since the opposition continued to hope that help would come from Moscow, Ulbricht decided, shortly after the bitter struggle between Khrushchev and his foes—Molotov, Kaganovich, and the others—had ended in June, 1957, to make his point more clearly, to strike at Schirdewan and his followers. Khrushchev had won, but only by a hair's breadth; Ulbricht knew it was a favorable moment in which to prejudice the Soviet leader against an "anti-Party group" in the SED. His attack was oblique, not head on. In October, 1957, Ulbricht first settled scores with Central Committee Secretaries Hager and Wandel, who had been "too soft" in 1956, although they had repented in the interim. At the close of the Central Committee plenary session, Ulbricht said, "It is our feeling that everything has not been brought out into the open in this discussion. The Central Committee's next meeting will probably have to be held in January, by which time everything will have been aired. I won't mention any names now. If names are wanted, those who wish to may add to my report at the next meeting of the Central Committee."

The day of reckoning for Ulbricht's real enemies thus appears to have been fixed as early as October, 1957, but Ulbricht evidently had trouble establishing proof of "factional activity" on their part. In December, he had a stroke of good luck: He learned that Selbmann and Ziller had criticized, even openly assailed, Party policy at a meeting with SED functionaries from the Wismut District. The Politburo took the attitude that "the extraordinarily grave events at this meeting point to factional activity going back a long time."

The Schirdewan "faction" was crushed at the thirty-fifth plenary meeting of the Central Committee in February, 1958. Ulbricht's years of crisis were over.

Ulbricht and the SED Opposition

All those who tried to overthrow Ulbricht shared certain motives, differed in others. But Ulbricht always followed the same rules in defeating his opponents. The three most important were:

1. *To play people off against each other.* Whenever a new anti-Ulbricht group was in the making, or was being smashed, former Ulbricht foes were given the chance to redeem themselves by fighting against it. Schirdewan helped to finish off Dahlem in 1953; Dahlem helped to destroy Schirdewan in 1958, taking the lead by describing Schirdewan's and Wollweber's "factional work" as a "crime against the Party" and by calling for the "harshest measures" against the accused. It was absolutely right and necessary, he said, to judge each individual by his "attitude toward the attack on Comrade

Ulbricht, since in attacking Ulbricht, the imperialist enemy was assaulting the Party." Ulbricht knew how to reward such servility: Dahlem was restored to his place on the Central Committee. All potential opponents of Ulbricht were brutally reminded that their patently hopeless struggle could only end in abject homage to the invincible leader. And they had to abandon their deluded hopes that Dahlem could be a "German Gomulka."

Ulbricht could pit groups as well as individuals against each other. Selbmann's chance remark, during Ulbricht's struggle with Schirdewan, that during the Nazi period, "some sat in prison and concentration camps, others talked over the radio," became a handy means of turning the personal contest of power into a clash between two groups of Party workers. This had been an obvious attack on the *émigrés*. Consequently, indignant and insulted, a number of prominent *émigrés* rallied to Ulbricht's side against the former concentration-camp inmates, among them Selbmann and Schirdewan.

2. *To nail down the support of Politburo members in periods of crisis and involve them as much as possible with the leader's own position.* Whenever Ulbricht's rivals were being openly condemned, other Party leaders had to give proof of their loyalty to the First Secretary. On the day that Schirdewan was stripped of office, for example, almost every Politburo member was forced publicly to praise Ulbricht as "the outstanding and most competent representative" of the SED. Then, to continue in Ulbricht's favor, Party leaders have to accept the fact that they are usually called upon to proclaim the especially unpopular measures deemed necessary by the First Secretary. When the Central Committee proposed to raise the work norms in May, 1953, Heinrich Rau had to defend the directive. When the Central Committee decided at the beginning of 1964 to condemn Professor Robert

Havemann's very popular philosophy lectures at Humboldt University, Politburo-Candidate Horst Sinderman was called upon to launch the attack. (Havemann was expelled from the SED in March and also stripped of his academic title.) The same technique is used when Ulbricht settles with his rivals; Matern made the accusation against Dahlem in 1953; Honecker did the honors against Schirdewan and Wollweber.

3. *When the rehabilitation of unjustly condemned Party leaders is necessary, to effect it silently and almost incidentally, while making any accusations or indictments of them as public as possible.* This was the case with Dahlem and Fechner. In this way, the impression is created that opposition to Ulbricht is doomed to failure, even when the accused has not engaged in any at all.

Though Ulbricht operated quite skillfully in the internal power struggles of the SED, he was often favored by circumstances over which he had no direct control. In other words, he has profited greatly from the basic dilemma of the SED opposition.

All of Ulbricht's opponents believed that they could win over the Soviet leaders to their side and convince them that Ulbricht was hurting the cause of Communism in Germany. There are grounds to believe that the Soviet Ambassador in East Berlin occasionally gave them hope or, at least, did not repulse them. But we do know that, at the crucial moment, the Kremlin always backed Ulbricht, either because the Soviets feared that Communist rule in Germany would be endangered by a change of leadership, or because Ulbricht had persuaded them of his support of Soviet interests in Germany. Since Ulbricht did emerge as victor in these struggles, the Party bureaucrats tended to remain neutral in each new battle until the outcome was clear.

And it is difficult for groups in opposition to Ulbricht to

find support among the people or, at least, within the ranks of the Party. There are technical reasons for this: the mass media—press, radio, television—are controlled by Ulbricht. No publisher would dare to print an open or disguised call for his dismissal. At Party Congresses, texts of speeches and discussions must be submitted beforehand, and there would be little point in departing from an approved speech to attack Ulbricht, since the delegates would be too frightened to react spontaneously and would tend to think they were witnessing an act of political hara-kiri by a desperate man who no longer cared what happened to him. The distrust that East Germans have toward the Party leaders is another factor, for it is not likely that they will find any given opponent to Ulbricht so very much more trustworthy than the man those opponents have served under for so long. Still, all the opposition groups and movements within the SED share a common imperative and a common goal: to win the people over to Communism.

This interpretation, though valid, has its limits. The Communist opposition in the D.D.R., whether its representatives are conscious of it or not, are subject to certain laws stronger than the possible motives of SED functionaries. When something first starts "buzzing" in their heads, when they begin to doubt current Party policy and speculate on how to improve things generally, then—sooner or later—they must, in order to be effective, take into account the demands and desires of the people. It is no accident that the search for a German perspective acceptable to the people played so large a part in the programs and plans of Zaisser and Herrnstadt, Harich and his friends, Schirdewan and his supporters. But precisely at this point the great dilemma and perhaps tragedy of the East German Communist opposition can be seen. A German perspective acceptable to the people would clash head-on with the interests of the Soviet Union. Were the SED opposition factions to gain Moscow's trust (for whatever reason), they would have a hard time gaining their desired support from the people. If their goal is an alliance with the people, and they accede to the wish for reunification, then conflict with the Soviet Union is, under present conditions, unavoidable.

VI

"Every true German wants reunification.
Our people cannot live without unity.
Saxony cannot exist without the Ruhr,
Bavaria without Saxony."
—WALTER ULBRICHT, *1946*

"Two hostile German states confront each
other on German soil today."
—SOCIALIST UNITY PARTY, NATIONAL
PROGRAM, *1962*

Ulbricht and Communist Policy on Germany

The Communist Exiles and Stalinist Policy on Germany

The Communist exiles who returned to Germany after World War II were determined not to repeat one of the worst errors they had made during the Weimar Republic, "underestimation of nationalism." They would be shrewder this time and adopt the sacred litany: "nation," "patriotism," "love of country." The *émigrés* had learned from Stalin, who had appealed to Russian patriotism during the "Great Patriotic War" and won tremendous popular support.

They also had their own experiences to draw on. Hitler had given them their first chance to represent the national interest without repudiating the class struggle; and the class enemy—Hitler and his supporters—had destroyed the German nation. The Communist *émigrés* intended to use this equation in the postwar situation. But who was now the national and class enemy?

The Communists themselves were also involved in a dual role. For how could they represent Soviet interests and simultaneously claim to be German patriots? The exiles believed they could resolve this contradiction according to a magic formula with whose help they would be able to conceal the Soviet-German conflict and create the illusion of harmonious Soviet-German interests. This magic formula concerned German unity.

Now it is true that both the Soviet Union and the Germans wanted a unified German nation. But it is also true that Moscow and the German Communist repatriates wanted a unified Germany in a Soviet sphere of influence. Stalin sought to extend the boundaries of the emerging Soviet empire beyond the Elbe to the Rhine. This, however, was not what the Germans wanted.

As things were, the impotent Germans could not block Stalin's drive for power in central Europe. The Western powers, Stalin's former allies, were the major obstacle. In consequence, the *émigrés* and their "friends"—it was customary in East German Communist circles, during the first years after the war, to refer to the Russians as "our friends" —decided to make American imperialism the new class and national enemy. American imperialism, they said, was responsible for Germany's division; it had taken over the fascist legacy. It was, so they said, the main enemy of the German nation. Consider it: In order to further their own imperialist plans, the Soviets were ready to revive that force which had almost caused their defeat—German nationalism; but now this force was to be directed not against them, but by them against the allies of yesterday. It was not difficult to make the new "main enemy of the Germans" into the "main enemy of the worker," for the Americans had opposed the plan for an Anti-fascist–Democratic order in West Germany (Stalin's instrument for establishing Communist influence in all Germany): There had been neither a merger of the KPD and SPD, nor industrial and land reforms in the American, English, and French occupation zones. On the contrary, the SED high command asserted, the oppressors of the working class had kept or regained key positions of power in West Germany and were now promoting the interests of American and English imperialism.

Stalin and his German henchmen must have known that the united Germany of which they spoke was already beyond reach even as the SED leaders called for a "popular movement against American imperialism" in the summer of 1949 and gave it organizational shape in the National Front for a Democratic Germany. The creation of the National Front, therefore, represents the beginning of the second phase in Communist policy on postwar Germany. The Soviet Union and the SED went on trying, of course, to drive a wedge between the Germans and the Western occupation powers by playing on nationalist feelings and nationalist desires for revenge. But their immediate goal now was to prevent or delay the entry of the West German Federal Republic into the Western defense alliance. This aim determined Communist policy on Germany until Stalin's death.

Ulbricht's View of the Federal Republic

During the first years after the war, Ulbricht said comparatively little in public on the German question. At Party Congresses, for example, the authoritative speeches on the subject were made by Pieck and Grotewohl; Ulbricht made his practical contribution through the "construction of the Anti-fascist–Democratic order" in the Soviet Zone. Not until he had been named General Secretary of the SED in 1950 did Ulbricht begin to speak more frequently on the German problem.

His speeches and articles from 1950 to 1952 are filled with diatribes against the Western occupation powers. For example, he wrote in *Pravda* in March, 1950, that "American imperialism is transforming West Germany into a colony and military staging ground."[1] A few months later, in July, 1950, he said, "A situation is developing in West Germany in which all strata of the population are beginning to fight colonization by U.S. imperialism . . . workers as well as employers, whom the United States is depriving of markets; and also peasants, who are in the grip of an agricultural crisis. . . . All segments of the population want to end this national enslavement."[2] He warned that "the ruling circles of the U.S., Great Britain, and France are preparing for war against the Soviet Union and its allies. They need the arms potential of the Ruhr, and German manpower as cannon-fodder." Their war preparations are accompanied "by the increasing impoverishment of the masses . . . by the insane reactionary offensive against the toilers, and the fascisization of all governments in the imperialist camp."[3] "The plan to crush the revolutionary proletariat, attempted in 1933 with the support of the American imperialists, has been revived and placed on the agenda for all Europe by the American gangsters."[4]

Soon after Stalin's death, the SED propaganda machine muted its tirades against "American imperialism" and the "ruling circles of Great Britain and France" and turned on a new "main enemy": "resurrected German imperialism." Actually, this theme had been introduced as early as July, 1951, when Ulbricht had said that the "main enemy of the national movement" is now "resurrected German imperialism." As "American imperialism's chief ally in Europe," it is preparing to remilitarize West Germany and wage war against the Soviet Union and the People's Democracies.[5] Meanwhile, the picture Ulbricht drew of conditions in the Federal Republic remained unchanged throughout the years:

In 1950, "the Bonn protectorate is forced to record growing unemployment from day to day."

In 1954, an "economic crisis" was imminent. "West German industry is chronically incapable of operating at full capacity. . . . This . . . is creating a large reserve army of permanent unemployed." Fifteen per cent of all registered jobless men were "completely destitute."

In 1955, "intensification of the class struggle" and "popular resistance" to the plans of the Federal Government was apparent.

In 1956, "signs of a political and cyclical economic crisis are multiplying in West Germany. The backlash will be felt soon." As was only to be expected, West German capitalists were trying to end these recurring political and economic crises and restore prosperity. But their solution was "greater exploitation."

In 1957, the German capitalists had borrowed "the most inhuman methods of exploitation" from the Americans and created "the most fearful system of exploitation that ever existed in Germany." The working masses were finally awakening: "It can be said that a sudden change has taken place in West Germany. . . . There has certainly . . . been a political turn."

In 1958, "a mass movement for an atom-free zone, for securing the peace," is developing in the Federal Republic, "because the people are beginning to see that the imperialist policy of the Adenauer Government is driving Germany to-

ward disaster." Still, "the working class and broad circles of
toilers in West Germany" should "regard the future with concern": They are forever being "sucked into capitalism's
periodic crises." It was different in the D.D.R.: "It is quite
clear that we [in the D.D.R.] are superior to West Germany
with respect to the social system, the rights of the workers and
the people, the administration of the economy, education, and
culture."

In 1959, the mood in West Germany was continuing to
change: Not just the working masses, but part of the West
German bourgeoisie as well were trying to shake off Adenauer's
rigid policies. The "Adenauer Government finds itself unable
to stem this shift in public opinion with its former means.
That is why it is sharpening the class struggle and resorting
to fascist methods . . . Adenauer is preparing for civil war
and fratricide. His *revanchist* policy is essentially like Hitler's, as presented in *Mein Kampf*."

In 1963, "What we [SED leaders] long predicted is now a
fact in West Germany . . . recurring government crises."[6]

Thus developed Ulbricht's analysis of the "deeper" meaning of the "German miracle." How could a state on the one
hand ravaged by so many periodic economic and political
crises, with its frightful system of exploitation, and on the
other, confronted by growing popular resistance and tottering
on the brink of civil war, survive at all, if not through a
miracle? We do not know whether Ulbricht believed what he
said about the Federal Republic. All we know is that he was
informed—mainly by KPD functionaries, specialists on West
German affairs, and SED agents who worked in the Federal
Republic. And it is unlikely that they had the courage to tell
their bosses that their side was failing while the enemy was
succeeding. Anti-Communism in the Federal Republic also
frequently leads one into seeing everything in the Soviet Zone

in the worst possible light. In any event, it is not surprising that functionaries so ideologically dependent on their Party will transform the class enemy's camp, doomed by the laws of history to destruction, into a fascist hell. Communist ideology insists: Man *cannot* prosper under capitalism. Besides, Ulbricht himself is equally circumscribed in terms of his necessary allegiances. The Soviet Union *expects* reports of successes. It may be hard for Ulbricht to admit that Communist propaganda in the Federal Republic has fallen on barren soil and that the goals of Communist policy in Germany are not being achieved. Not only false information but his own ideological obsessions cause his unrealistic views and policies.

Ulbricht's Policies on Germany and Berlin in the Post-Stalin Era

In Stalin's lifetime, the Kremlin alone shaped Communist policy on Germany: The SED was, therefore, a minor executive agency. But Stalin's successors gave more responsibility and initiative to Communist Party leaders in the satellite countries, and, in many instances, they allowed them a voice in decision-making, a change that was strengthened by the Soviet-Chinese conflict. The SED high command now found it possible to exert more influence on Communist policy concerning Germany and Berlin. Ulbricht does not make important decisions in this sphere even today—his scope is greater in domestic affairs—but he can make proposals, express doubts, join in the discussion. If Moscow and Pankow had an identical German policy while Stalin lived, but differences of opinion subsequently emerged, how is one to characterize Stalin's last venture in German policy in the spring of 1952? Did Stalin act then in the interests of the SED leadership?

Just ten weeks before Chancellor Adenauer signed the European Defense Community (EDC) Treaty, on March 10, 1952, the Soviet Union made a new proposal to the three Western powers. It was "promptly to take up the question of a peace treaty with Germany" and to agree on the conditions "that would favor the speediest formation of an all-German government expressing the will of the German people." The Western powers replied to this note on March 25. This first exchange of notes was followed by three more, the last in September.[7] The differences that determined the failure of them all, however, were already fully expressed in the first:

1) The Western powers demanded that a U.N. commission supervise all-German elections that would precede formation of an all-German government; the Soviet Union, on the other hand, wanted the four occupation powers jointly to establish such a supervisory commission.*

2) The Soviet Union declared Germany's frontiers as drawn at the Potsdam Conference to be final; the Western powers wanted final decision on the borders reserved for a peace conference.

3) The Soviet Union insisted that a reunified Germany could not be permitted "to join any coalitions or military alliances directed against any state that had fought Germany in the war." The Western powers replied that they were convinced of the need "for a policy of European unity" and therefore supported plans that "assure Germany's participation in a purely defensive European community."

* The United Nations General Assembly had adopted a resolution on December 20, 1951, to send a commission composed of delegates from Brazil, Ireland, the Netherlands, Pakistan, and Poland, to the D.D.R., the Federal Republic, and West Berlin in order to investigate whether conditions were favorable for holding free and secret elections. On January 18, 1952, Poland declared that it would not participate. In March, the Federal Republic and West Berlin declared themselves ready to provide the commission with all the support necessary for its work.

One thing is certain: Stalin had tried unsuccessfully to block West Germany's entry into a military alliance with his former allies. But had he been truly willing to pay the price that would have prevented it—agreeing to reunification? Did Stalin consider a reunited, neutral Germany between the two big power blocs more important than Communist rule between the Oder and Elbe rivers? If so, did Ulbricht and the other SED leaders agree? Adenauer's signing of the EDC Treaty relieved the Communists of the need to prove that their offer had been seriously meant. Indeed, Stalin did not even wait for ratification of the treaty; for all practical purposes, he dropped the offer during the summer. Ignoring Germany's national interests, Stalin decided immediately to Bolshevize the D.D.R. and to hasten its incorporation into the Eastern bloc. At the Second SED Party Conference in July, 1952, Ulbricht suddenly proclaimed the "construction of Socialism in the D.D.R." This Socialist construction, he said, would favorably affect "the struggle for Germany's reunification" and was a direct preparation for all-German elections. The population of the Federal Republic was summoned to a "struggle for national liberation against the American, English, and French occupation powers" and to "overthrow the vassal regime in Bonn"—a necessary condition for establishing German unity. "National military forces of the D.D.R.," Ulbricht said, would give powerful support and courage to the revolutionary mass movement in West Germany. These violent words could hardly convince West German foes of the EDC Treaty that the earlier Soviet proposals had been in earnest. Instead, they only strengthened the case of those who argued for immediate, close ties with the West in view of the threat of Communist aggression.

Given Ulbricht's conduct in the months before and after Stalin's death, it is likely that in 1952 he was already one of those Communist leaders who favored a German Communist rump-state in the Eastern bloc over the "all-German experiment." It is hard to see why he fought so bitterly against the views of Beria and Malenkov, unless his views on German policy were based on the single premise that Communist rule in the D.D.R. must never be questioned or attacked. Ulbricht feared that Beria and Malenkov might also use Communist "achievements" in his sphere of power in the Soviet Zone as possible bartering points to reduce international tensions*; perhaps they might place Stalin's offer of March, 1952, on the bargaining table as well. Ulbricht decided, therefore, to fight. For the first time since the end of World War II, a fundamental conflict of interests had erupted between Ulbricht and Moscow, a development that was sure to influence Ulbricht's relations with Nikita Khrushchev. But by 1955 at the latest, Khrushchev had adopted Ulbricht's premise that Communist rule in the D.D.R. was not negotiable, and basic agreement on the German question had been restored.

In 1954, the SED began to tone down its propaganda for free German elections. After the Geneva Summit Conference in October, 1955, Ulbricht for the first time openly rejected the proposal for all-German elections under prevailing conditions, insisting that the SED would agree to them only after the Federal Republic left NATO, the Western occupation powers departed German soil, and "democratic relations" were introduced in West Germany—the nationalization of basic industries, reforms on the East German model in agriculture and education, and the replacement of all "militarists

---

* In a speech of March 8, 1963, Khrushchev said: "Together with Malenkov, Beria . . . proposed to liquidate the D.D.R. as a Socialist State. They advised the SED to withdraw the slogan of the struggle for Socialism. The Party's Central Committee indignantly rejected these traitorous proposals and struck the provocateurs a crushing blow." (*Neues Deutschland,* March 14, 1963.)

and imperialists" along with their "agents" in the state apparatus with "honest democrats" drawn from the toiling masses.*

The goal of Communist policy in Germany was now diplomatic recognition of the D.D.R. "One Germany does not exist. . . . At present, there are two German states," declared Ulbricht. "Everything else is unimportant."[8] True, Ulbricht's proposal of January, 1957, for an all-German Council that would exercise functions of government, pave the way for a unified administration, and prepare for all-German elections was a device to intensify the break, not heal it, for he insisted that the basis for federation be the recognition of the "D.D.R.'s accomplishments" and the transformation of the Federal Republic along "Anti-fascist–Democratic" lines.[9]

Once Ulbricht and the SED leaders had said that two states existed on German soil, they had to be consistent and revise their earlier attitude on Berlin. In January, 1949, even while the Berlin blockade was on, Ulbricht had said: "We do not consider Berlin an East Zone city or province, but the capital of Germany." But if a united Germany no longer existed, Berlin could no longer be its capital.

---

* This first statement appeared in an article-supplement to *Neues Deutschland*, November 1, 1955. A year later, Ulbricht put it this way: "It would be foolish to talk generally about all-German elections as long as the West German arms millionaires, the Hitler Generals, and other war-thirsty forces are in a position to use their economic power to influence the elections. . . . Since the Adenauer government is unprepared and incapable of taking the peaceful road to reunification because it depends on the arms monopolies and the militaristic cliques . . . the real conditions for reunification will probably not exist until the West German population . . . ousts the Adenauer government and creates a regime that is ready, together with the East German Parliament and the Government of the D.D.R., to solve national problems in a peaceful manner." ("Die Voraussetzungen für die friedliche Wiedervereinigung Deutschlands" ["The Bases for Peaceful Reunification of Germany"], *Zur Geschichte der deutschen Arbeiterbewegung*, VI, 178–79.)

According to a former high SED official, the Berlin question loomed large in SED policy as early as 1956–57. But one factor superseded their own ideas and wishes on that issue—i.e., the constant stream of East German residents fleeing to the West. Year after year, thousands of men and women left East Germany for the Federal Republic via West Berlin, and it was obviously impossible to stem this tide. The Party leaders knew that as long as the West Berlin escape-hatch remained open, the best they could hope for was fewer escapes. It is said that during the Hungarian revolution in 1956, SED leaders proposed to the Soviet ambassador in East Berlin seizing West Berlin by surprise attack.

They must have counted on the protest meeting planned in West Berlin against Soviet intervention in Hungary; excitable youngsters would mass at the Brandenburg Gate and then march on to the Soviet Embassy on Unter den Linden; it was a certainty that the demonstrators would smash the Embassy's windows and create a stir. This would give Soviet troops a legitimate excuse to march into West Berlin, and with them would go the D.D.R. army. There was no reason to fear war; the *coup* would be eclipsed by the general excitement over Hungarian events and the Suez crisis. But Ambassador Pushkin turned the plan down. Ulbricht then worked out a new plan and presented it to the Soviet Union in January, 1957— to proclaim all Berlin the capital of the D.D.R. Khrushchev continued to turn down proposals of this kind: The four-power status of Berlin was not to be violated.*

Ulbricht seems to have remained as obsessed as before with

* Unfortunately, there are no known facts to substantiate this report. However, that January, 1957, may have been the crucial period makes a good deal of sense. At the thirtieth plenum of the Central Committee, at the end of January, 1957, Ulbricht announced the confederation plan. This project must have been discussed beforehand with Moscow, in all probability during a conference between the Russians and SED leaders on January 4–9 in Moscow.

the need to stop the flights from the D.D.R. In May, 1957, he threatened:

> West Berliners know that West Berlin lies within the German Democratic Republic. The ties of the agents of imperialism and NATO propaganda extend into West Berlin, but NATO's military power will never extend that far. . . . The West Berlin situation has sharpened since West Germany became part of NATO and West Berlin a center for the operations of NATO agents against the D.R.R. as well as a radar base. Everyone understands that West Berlin's population may some day have to pay very dearly.[10]

In the autumn of 1953, Khrushchev finally yielded to the continued SED demands for a solution to the Berlin problem. On October 28, the eve of elections in West Berlin, Ulbricht, with the Kremlin's consent, repeated: "All of Berlin lies in the territory of the D.D.R. . . . The Western powers have destroyed the legal basis for their presence in Berlin; they no longer have any legal, moral, or political justification for their continued occupation of West Berlin."[11] On November 10, Khrushchev supported Ulbricht in a speech at Moscow. On November 27, the Soviet Government handed the three Western powers notes demanding that West Berlin be transformed into a demilitarized free city, with a limit of six months set to negotiations over the proposal. With this threat once made, however, the Soviet Union did nothing to worsen the crisis when the ultimatum ran out on May 27, 1959, undoubtedly realizing they had been wrong to believe, as Ulbricht had encouraged them to do, that the West would retreat. Relative calm prevailed during the next two years, until the early summer of 1961, and Ulbricht waited apparently in vain for a "solution to the Berlin problem."

Then, on June 15, 1961, the East Berlin Press Office invited a large number of foreign and German journalists to a

press conference with Walter Ulbricht. "Ladies and gentlemen," said the Chairman of the State Council, "a peace
treaty with Germany and the solution of the West Berlin
question are on the agenda for 1961, as everybody knows."
One West Berlin newspaper woman asked whether a D.D.R.
state boundary line was going to be drawn at the Brandenburg Gate. Ulbricht answered:

> I interpret your question to mean that there are men in West
> Germany who would like to mobilize the construction workers
> of the D.D.R. capital to build a wall. I have no knowledge of
> any such plan. The construction workers of our capital are
> primarily engaged in building houses and that absorbs most
> of their labor. No one has any intention of putting up a wall.
> I have already said in the past: We are for the peaceful settle-
> ment of relations between West Berlin and the Government of
> the German Democratic Republic. This is the simplest and
> most normal way to settle these problems.[12]

Eight weeks later, on August 13, 1961, the Berlin Wall
went up. Had Ulbricht changed his mind in the interim? His
statement in June (no one, after all, had mentioned a wall),
as well as Khrushchev's remark to the former Ambassador of
the Federal Republic of Germany in Moscow, Dr. Kroll, indi-
cate that Ulbricht was interested in a "peaceful settlement,"*
that is, in concluding a separate peace treaty between the
Soviet Union and the D.D.R., but that Khrushchev opposed
such a step and decided in favor of the Wall.

A speech given by Ulbricht three days before the Wall was
built reveals clearly why he so badly wanted the peace treaty:

> A peace treaty with the German Democratic Republic must
> result in a new settlement of the West Berlin question; obvi-

---

* Dr. Kroll has requested me to treat the details of this talk confiden-
tially. I have, therefore, limited myself to this bare reference.

ously, the treaty will put an end, throughout the entire territory of the German Democratic Republic (of which West
Berlin is a part) to all occupation rights and the West Berlin
occupation statute. When the peace treaty is concluded, the
German Democratic Republic will exercise its sovereign rights
to the full, including those rights temporarily left to the Soviet
Union in 1955. These deal with the control of persons and
vital goods moving across the D.D.R. territory to supply the
Western garrisons in West Berlin.[13]

In other words, with the help of a peace treaty between
the Soviet Union and the D.D.R., Ulbricht intended to control traffic to and from West Berlin and to drive the Western
powers from the city. He was a man in a hurry. There was
no reason, he said, to postpone signing the treaty: "The German people will most certainly be dragged into a new war
if there is any delay in the peace treaty. . . . It is the national
obligation of the German working class . . . to conclude the
peace treaty today—not tomorrow or the day after that. . . .
It must take place now! Time has run out."

Even after the Wall was built, Ulbricht continued his prod-
ding. In several speeches during September, 1961, he spoke
of "signing the treaty this year" or "in the months immediately ahead." And while Khrushchev, at the Twenty-second
Congress of the CPSU in October, 1961, indicated the actual
signing date was, under certain conditions, of secondary importance—"If the Western powers show themselves ready to
settle the German problem, the question of when a German
peace treaty is to be signed will not have such importance. We
would not then insist that the peace treaty has to be signed
by December 31, 1961"—Ulbricht, on the other hand, asserted
that the Western powers wanted only to gain time, but that
the D.D.R. was determined "to conclude a peace treaty as
soon as possible."[14]

These differences over precisely how urgent the peace treaty was continued until early 1963, but Ulbricht did not succeed in converting the Soviet Union to his point of view. Khrushchev had realized that the large-scale flight of people could no longer be tolerated—that had been "solved" by building the Wall—but he was not prepared to hand Ulbricht the power of decision over war or peace. Ulbricht continued to try to convince the Soviet Union that a peace treaty would not lead to war, but for Khrushchev, the risk of military conflict with the West was too great. He went on placating Ulbricht with promises of signing the treaty, but also went on postponing the final date for signature. The so-called treaty of friendship concluded in 1964 between the U.S.S.R. and the D.D.R. was, as far as Ulbricht is concerned, not a satisfactory substitute for the peace treaty.

However, today it looks as if the new men in the Kremlin and Ulbricht are agreed on what the general Communist perspective should be on Germany. No basic changes were made on it after Ulbricht unfolded his confederation plan in January, 1957; the plan was only modified on some points or polished up for propaganda purposes. The "national program" or "national document" presented by Ulbricht on behalf of the Central Committee to the National Front for a Democratic Germany in 1962 rests on the principle that "two basically different and completely independent states" exist "in hostile confrontation." On one side is the "West Zone State . . . created by the U.S. imperialists and West German finance capitalists to divide Germany . . . an imperialist, antinational state structure forced on the West German population and ruled by men who are guided only by the profit interests of the finance capitalists and the *revanchist* interests of the Hitler Generals." On the other side, there is the "peace-loving German Democratic Republic, which is in full accord with the progressive laws of human society." It cannot postpone the "fulfillment of its historic mission, the completion of Socialist construction, until the peace-loving forces in West Germany under working class leadership have become victorious." The German Democratic Republic would sin against the German people and their future were it to make its development dependent on events in West Germany. It cannot wait until "the people [there] take their fate into their hands" and clear the road for reunification by creating an "Antifascist–Democratic West Germany."

The "national program" therefore calls on the two hostile states "to live peacefully together" and establish "peaceful coexistence" in central Europe. The most suitable form, therefore, would be a German confederation in which Berlin could join "as a demilitarized, free, and neutral city." This confederation would agree on "complete disarmament in Germany, the prohibition of atomic and nuclear weapons on German soil, and the neutrality of both German states."*

---

* These points were made in Ulbricht's speech on the forty-fifth anniversary of the founding of the KPD, *Neues Deutschland*, January 4, 1964. On the subject of confederation, the program adopted at the Sixth Party Congress says:

"The formation of a German confederation can come about only through the creation of a minimum of correct relations and understandings between the D.D.R., the West German Federal Republic, and the Free City of West Berlin. . . . The confederation rests on the sovereignty and equal status of both states and the free state of West Berlin. It does not establish any continuing central authority and calls for no changes in their respective social systems. The organs of confederation consult and decide upon recommendations to the parliaments and governments of the participants in the confederation. These recommendations have the following aims: to secure lasting peace for the German people; to execute the terms of the peace treaty; to prohibit nuclear weapons and carriers of nuclear weapons; gradual withdrawal of both German states from military obligations resulting from membership in different power groupings; military neutrality and complete disarmament; to coordinate collaboration of the two confederation members in the work of international organizations; to create and expand normal relations between both German states, as well as between the D.D.R. and West Berlin, in the spheres of economics, trade, culture, science, technology, and sports."

Ulbricht explained in 1963 that even before the confederation was founded, joint commissions could be set up by both governments to "work out and transmit to both regimes proposals on trade, culture, science, movements of people and goods, and monetary exchanges."[15] The proposal on commissions was new; so was the fact that Ulbricht and the other SED leaders subsequently began to take a somewhat more realistic view of the Federal Republic. They admit the Communists have no chance at present "to kindle the flames of popular resistance" and overthrow the West German government. Ulbricht's latest formulation, that the Federal Republic is "an economically strong state ruled by authoritarian methods," sounds more moderate than previous pronouncements.[16]

Ulbricht and his clique often speak of the "two completely independent states on German soil"—naturally, since they want the D.D.R. recognized as a state in its own right. But the SED's policy, and its standing in Moscow, is peculiarly bound up with the stability of the Federal Republic. The Kremlin measures Ulbricht's economic policies by the economic situation in the Federal Republic; in 1958, Ulbricht announced that the "chief economic task" in the next three years was to prove "unambiguously the superiority of the Socialist system in the D.D.R. over the dominant imperialist forces in Bonn." The plan designed to achieve this goal failed. Although Moscow's order—"to demonstrate Socialism's superiority over capitalism" in competition with the Federal Republic—continues to occupy a priority position in SED policy, Ulbricht has failed to carry it out.

VII

"It is contrary to the spirit of Marxism-
Leninism to elevate someone and make
an idol of him, to transform him into
a person who supposedly knows all, sees
all, thinks for all, who can do all and is
completely infallible."
—NIKITA KHRUSHCHEV, *at the Twentieth Congress of the Communist
Party of the Soviet Union*

The Chairman of the Council of State

Ulbricht as Father of His People

In the spring of 1961, a kindergarten teacher in the town of Fürstenwalde was wondering how she could communicate the proper admiration for Walter Ulbricht to her charges. One morning, she put a picture of the Chairman of the Council of State on display. She reported her intentions, experiences, and successes as follows:

Goal: To familiarize the children with the picture of the Chairman of the Council of State; to pronounce his name correctly for them; to have them listen attentively to what I say and make them feel he is a good man.

Topic: Looking at the picture of our State Council Chairman.

Method: Looking at the picture and saying his name. I tell them: "Walter Ulbricht is a wonderful man. He was a worker. Bernie's father, Angela's mother, Mrs. Müller, I, and all good people like him. He looks after us." Then we practice pronouncing his name. (Some children say Ullrich!) I hang the picture on the wall and place flowers in a vase next to it—to teach the children that we should always have fresh flowers in front of this good man's portrait.

Evaluation: The children listen very attentively. All of them, right down to the youngest one, pronounce his name correctly. I have the impression of having awakened their first positive feelings toward Walter Ulbricht.

This first success encouraged the kindergarten teacher. She decided to go a step farther: The children were to recognize the State Council Chairman in other pictures. An opportunity soon arose. On May 1, the streets of the town were decorated and Ulbricht's picture was widely displayed. The children were overjoyed to see the portrait outside their kindergarten room, but they came back to the schoolroom with a mistaken notion: "Some of the children said there were 'many Walter Ulbrichts.' "

This report, taken from the East Berlin journal *New Education in the Kindergarten,*[1] is just one example of the attempts to popularize Ulbricht as the father of his country. Ulbricht took on this additional "office" in the fall of 1960. Wilhelm Pieck, President of East Germany, had died in September, and the Party leadership had seized on the opportunity afforded by his death to change the constitution and replace the President by a so-called Council of State, elected by parliament for a four-year period and consisting of a chairman, six deputy chairmen, sixteen members, and a secretary. According to the new constitution, the Council of State proclaims the laws, ratifies and revokes international treaties, and performs all functions customarily associated with the supreme organ of a state. In addition, it can give its decisions the force of law, has final say on basic questions of defense and security, approves directives of the National Defense Council* (of which Ulbricht is chairman) and appoints its members, and is empowered to issue "binding interpretations of the laws." Although this new Council has been granted many rights by the constitution, its political significance should not be overestimated. Its members are not the most powerful officials in the D.D.R.

The most important post in the Council is that of Chairman, and history proves that the position has been tailored to Ulbricht's needs. The constitution emphasizes that he is not *primus inter pares,* but in fact *directs* the work of the Council. He signs the laws, swears in newly appointed government officials, and designates ambassadors and envoys. He is also authorized to proclaim a "state of emergency" should he decide the country is in danger of attack.

Ulbricht has created an institution that allows him to unite Party and state power in one person, to act as chief of state and to satisfy his desire to be honored as father of his country in this "first Workers' and Peasants' State."

Accession to his new, additional office changed Ulbricht's personal way of life only little. He and his wife had moved into a new housing development for the Party élite before he became Chairman. Its construction in the beautiful woodland

* The National Defense Council was established by a law of February 10, 1960. It organizes and implements "the defense of the Workers' and Peasants' State and the Socialist victories of the working masses."

area north of Berlin between Wandlitz and Basdorf was planned at the start of the 1950's, but the costly project was delayed after the 1953 revolt and the Twentieth Congress of the CPSU; it was finally finished in 1960.

This restricted area is cut off from the outside world by a high wall made of concrete blocks, which is lit up at night. Just outside the wall are situated the small, plain houses of the servants and members of the security guard. Within the wall stand the two-story houses occupied by Ulbricht, Premier Stoph, Hermann Matern, Minister of Justice; Hilde Benjamin, the President of the parliament; Dieckmann, and other members of the D.D.R. élite. Each house has ten or twelve rooms and is furnished to the taste of its occupant. The décor of the Ulbricht house is fairly modest. The SED boss had only two special wishes: Chinese silk wall hangings in one of the rooms and Venetian mosaic flooring in another.

The élite have their own community center; it contains a banquet hall, restaurant, bar, movie theater, swimming pool, and library. There are also massage rooms, barber shops, beauty salons, a kindergarten, and a doctor's office. Adjacent to it are a rifle range and a tennis court.

Health permitting, Ulbricht begins his working day with calisthenics. Dressed in gym pants and a sports shirt, he does ten minutes of setting-up exercises or takes a short trot through the woods. He leaves for Berlin at about 9 A.M.; his office is in Niederschönhausen Castle.

Since he has become head of state, Ulbricht makes frequent visits to towns and villages throughout East Germany. He is always accompanied on these trips by security guards, and sweeping security measures are taken in every locality he visits. Three days before he was to lay the cornerstone of a building in Leipzig, for example, the construction site was carefully inspected by the security police, about 25,000 bricks were cleared away, and searchlights were set up so that the building could be lighted continually during the nights preceding the ceremony. On the day of Ulbricht's visit, a large contingent of People's Police blocked off the construction site; all workers in a nearby building that overlooked it were "evacuated." The liquor bottle traditionally "broken" at these ceremonies had to be given to the security police, who supplied a substitute one.

Ulbricht's secretary, Gotsche, has given the official reasons for these frequent trips in his description of Ulbricht's visit to the Northern District of the D.D.R.:

A large conference was held at Rostock on improving work in the fishing industry; captains of the fleet, coastal fishermen, scientists, and officials from the shipyards were present. . . . [Comrade Ulbricht's] intervention led to important changes. Drydocking and repair intervals were reduced, new fishing methods were approved and introduced. As a result, the catches increased and there was more food in many homes. This was the outcome of the first day on his itinerary.

The second day was spent at the Institute for Plant Cultivation in Gross-Lüsewitz. . . . Walter Ulbricht met with the Republic's outstanding expert on animal fodder, Professor Schick, and his colleagues. . . . Walter Ulbricht's next destination was Krien-Krusenfelde-Albinshof. . . . In these agricultural villages, Walter Ulbricht proved that the food needs of the population would be well taken care of once all managers and workers of cooperatives adopted the competitive method of work. He spoke with peasants of both sexes, with plowing and cattle-breeding brigades, with young tractor-drivers and old peasants whose weather-beaten faces lit up in assent when Walter Ulbricht asked whether the quotas would be met. Before going on to Lemmersdorf, in the Strasburg District, he visited the oil-drilling area in the Grimmen District. Why? Because oil, the development of the petroleum industry, is one of the most important problems in the economy of the German Democratic Republic. Comrade Ulbricht spoke with oil-drillers, geologists, engineers, and technicians. . . . In his speeches at Lemmersdorf, he sketched the ambitious program and perspectives of Socialist agriculture. . . . Later, at the great agricultural exhibition in Markkleeberg, he summed up the results of his trip. . . .

This is the way Walter Ulbricht works. It is the secret of his expert knowledge which technically qualifies him to speak on all concrete questions, the source of his creativity. . . . And in the late evening, when all are worn out from the cares of the day, he "makes his rounds," takes his evening stroll, though it may be storming or snowing.[2]

But Ulbricht's visits are not just concerned with competition among collective-farm peasants, production figures, the oil industry, or fishing hauls. They are also designed to create an image of the head of state. Feature articles by the SED journalists who accompany Ulbricht on his trips were reminiscent of accounts given by courtiers of the travels of their prince. One journalist writes:

"A fine man," you hear a woman worker say, after the State Council Chairman, accompanied by his wife and surrounded by a swarm of newspaper, television, and radio reporters, wishes good luck to a work brigade. The waves of good feeling rise high on this Friday afternoon. Hearty greetings are exchanged, handshakes . . . applause. . . . I'm a trifle annoyed only at a television reporter who has a long cable dragging behind him and keeps stumbling on the heels of our important guest. The latter perspires, but the words he speaks into the microphone are full of genuine enthusiasm. . . . It is refreshing to hear the friendly conversations between the workers and the highest representative of our state. . . . The school orchestra is about to strike up the tune "Free Youth, New Life." Ulbricht's comment is, "It rings out in the valley, in the factory, everywhere."[3]

The official Party newspaper, *Neues Deutschland,* reports in
a similar vein:

> So many cares still oppress our citizens. But a man sits up
> there in the Presidium to whom we can tell all this frankly and
> freely. . . . Problems that seemed insoluble immediately turn
> out to be simple. People breathe freely, laugh freely, and are
> inspired. "Our road is hard, of course it is hard, we don't hide
> the fact. But it is leading to good times for our people and
> that's what counts." The way he says this makes us want to
> shout with enthusiasm and, by the same token, to creep into a
> mousehole because there have been times when some of us
> have lacked faith.[4]

Are we to believe the SED journalists? Are all of Ulbricht's trips "genuine triumphal processions of joy and enthusiasm" which express "the love and faith of the people"?
This "universally honored" man has also permitted or ordered citizens to be brought before the courts and sentenced
for making uncomplimentary remarks about him. In 1958,
a dentist by the name of Dr. Föst was condemned to one year
in prison because he had publicly (in a restaurant) referred
to Ulbricht as "the goatee," and that, said the court, defamed
the state. "I am not omniscient like Walter Ulbricht," Herbert
Gaedecke replied to a question from one of his pupils in a
technical vocational school. He too was convicted of defam-
ing the state and sent to jail for six months. Wolfgang Steinke,
a member of the Central Committee, remarked, "Anyone who
agitates against Walter Ulbricht is continuing the murderous
activities of the Nazi gangsters during the fascist period
against the workers' movement. He will . . . get a taste not
only of our better arguments, but of our strength and fists
as well."[5]

Herbert Gaedecke was sent to jail, but he could justly have
pleaded that Ulbricht himself tries to create an impression

of omniscience. Besides airing his views on agricultural methods, the best ways to catch herring, production plans, problems of foreign trade, etc., the Chairman also talks about art, architecture, and sports.

On Ulbricht's seventieth birthday, the painter Otto Nagel described Ulbricht as an "unsettling viewer of art" who made it difficult for the artists and critics who guide him on his visits through art exhibitions. "Just when you feel sure of yourself, he suddenly bursts out with a question, 'Well, what does the working class get out of that? How does this art help our toilers in the struggle? What does it give them?' " Professor Lea Grundig explained this approach as a product of "Walter Ulbricht's quick capacity to grasp . . . the ideological weaknesses of a work of art."[6] Professor Bernhard Heisig was one victim of this talent. He entered a painting on "Parisian Communards Conversing and Resting" in a Leipzig art exhibition; Ulbricht looked at the picture and concluded that it did not portray this historic event realistically: "The Communards stormed the heavens, they did not loll about. This painting is proof that we still have an ideological job to do in art."[7]

Ulbricht's preoccupation with architecture is also ideological. It is one of the former cabinetmaker's special hobbyhorses: "In laying out the different parts of the city we must not take the narrow, closed-in architectural forms of the capitalist period as our guide. The boxlike houses on the American model being built in West Berlin, Frankfurt-am-Main, Stuttgart, and Hamburg are a complete break with our national traditions."[8]

Directives for Socialist architecture also go into minute detail. When architects drew up plans for Stalinallee—later renamed Karl Marx Allee—in East Berlin, they proposed placing the entrances to the buildings on the side streets and in the gardens. "Ulbricht stubbornly fought to have the entrances on Stalinallee itself, pointing out the enormous impression that entering a house makes on a person. . . . He described the entries to castles and patrician houses, and demanded that the architects give the same importance to the entrances of workers' apartment buildings."⁹

Ulbricht applies these same few formulas, slightly modified, to every field. He tells the architects to study Marxism-Leninism in order to build correctly; he advises the painters that "ideology is the basis of artistic representation"; he enlightens the athletes: "Success in the sports movement depends in large part on the athlete's ideology." Another formula always cropping up in Ulbricht's speeches can be phrased as follows: "Learn from the Soviet Union; the best and most progressive achievements are made there. Reject everything that comes out of the Federal Republic." Athletes, too, must systematically apply "the scientific experiences that have been assimilated in the Soviet Union." One cannot learn anything about sports from the Federal Republic, Ulbricht says, because athletes there are "controlled by the Bonn Government, a monopoly capitalist regime," serve to "maintain labor power for the benefit of capitalist exploitation," and are "organized by the state to further the goals of NATO policy." In the D.D.R., sports are different. They are "Socialist in content," they serve to foster international recognition of the rump-state, the activist workers' movement, and the "struggle for peace," and they should be considered a "patriotic duty."

Ulbricht, like many other Communist leaders, enjoys taking a position on everything. As long as the Party claims to be omniscient and infallible, it is only logical for its highest representatives to act as if they knew everything. But when the Communist Party begins to call for technical experts, when it finally admits that an individual with the "correct" ideology cannot necessarily build a house, then the know-it-all assumptions of its leaders begin to sound ludicrous.

Ulbricht's compulsion to speak out on everything was obvious even before he became Chairman of the Council of State. But once he assumed this job, he permitted—or, more probably, ordered—a cult of personality to spring up around him. There is nothing like it in the rest of the Eastern bloc, and it evokes memories of Stalin even among the friendliest of critics.

This cult finds expression in many songs and poems, like the ones by Becher and Gotsche below, that endlessly repeat the same themes:

> In your voice, we still hear ring
> Karl Liebknecht's 'in spite of everything,'
> Thälmann's fearless gaze
> Peers from your face.

Or:

> He was present when the new Party was born.
> And knew Karl Liebknecht and Rosa.
> He was there when we went to Lenin
> And he was with Thälmann, too.
> And when our old songs ring out
>   Telling of the Party, he is at our side!

In his poem "Comrade Walter Ulbricht," the young poet Horst Solomon has included almost every important SED propaganda theme:

> Still young in years,
> You studied the class struggle.
> Later you marched with passionate
> Heart under Thälmann's banner.

And as night wrapped Germany in her shroud
And the "brown shirts," the butcher shirt,
Filled the world with horror;

As the people of this gagged earth
Lost their faith in Goethe and Schiller,
You and a handful of comrades gave birth
To the New Germany.

Soon there was bread
And butter and shoes.
The Republic was flourishing
When the enemy—it was June 17—
Filled confused brains with lies and nonsense.
The swastika leered insolently
In the lapels of the putschists.
"Down with the Workers! The Peasants' power!"
The Fascists roared.
But you stood firm, Comrade Ulbricht,
With Stalingrad courage.
We were stronger and we crushed
The "White Guard" spawn.

Comrade Ulbricht
You hold Ernst Thälmann's legacy
In your loyal hands.
Whoever defames you
Wants to slander us—
The Party and the class.
There is no "but";
There is no "if."
Either one understands this
Or, stupid and blinded,
Falls victim to the enemy.
You stand at the summit of our Party,
Have given your best to her.

She was and is your heart, your blood,
And your life.

With love and great understanding
You have taught us how to think
as Party people should.
You kept the banner pure;
The Schirdewans were swept out
"unceremoniously."

Comrade Ulbricht,
A day will come
When you will speak
At our Party Congress:
Socialism is on the march
On the Howaldt docks,
In Bavaria,
And the Ruhr mines.

Other writers voice their feelings for Ulbricht in prose.
One article, written by two functionaries of the Central Committee, described Ulbricht as an "outstanding Socialist leader type" with the following traits: perseverance, energy, intelligence, perspicacity, politeness, great political experience and expertise in many fields, an intimate knowledge of life, simplicity and modesty, respect and love for the creative individual, a receptive attitude toward the opinions and proposals of working people, patience and comradely help in overcoming difficulties, a firm will to do everything that serves the people's interests, dedication to educating people to think for themselves. . . . Other Ulbricht admirers wish to go beyond words and express their feelings in deeds. The Association of House Gardeners and Breeders of Small Domestic Fowls and Animals reported in 1963: "The members of our Association are increasing the amount of leisure time

they spend on their gardens and on birds and animals—in the production of fruits and vegetables, eggs, meat, honey, milk, wool, and pelts—as a way of honoring Walter Ulbricht."

A look at the East German press, especially in the months after the Berlin Wall was erected (at that time, newspapers published testimonials of loyalty to Ulbricht almost daily), will quickly convince the reader that the Fürstenwald teacher who inspired her pupils with love of the Chairman was acting on orders. In late 1961 and early 1962, the educational authorities sent instructions throughout the country on how to familiarize the children and students with that "great model," Ulbricht. Children are brainwashed not only in the classroom, but also at meetings of the Young Pioneers. Through illustrative examples, they are supposed to be taught that Ulbricht is "a good German" and the "greatest living German workers' leader." "Special displays for Comrade Walter Ulbricht" must be set up in schools and kindergartens—decorated with a red cloth, with a portrait, flowers, and mottoes such as "We love our Republic." Or, "With Walter Ulbricht for Germany's happiness."

Inevitably, the population began to accuse the SED of fostering a Stalinist cult of personality around Ulbricht. But the SED leadership hastened to say that popular faith in and love of a leader "were not identical with the cult of personality. The condemnation of the cult of personality did not obviate the need to honor deserving leaders."[10]

The Communists denounce "the cult of personality" in order to deflect criticism from their system to an individual, Stalin. But it would be accurate to apply this notion to the Ulbricht cult. The latter is a form of twentieth-century byzantinism, which has been fostered in its time by Stalin as well as Hitler, Tito as well as Nkrumah. The motives of the SED leadership are easy to explain. Ulbricht is the most hated man in Germany. He is a convenient channel through which many people discharge their hatred for and disgust with Communism. The Party functionaries find it necessary to glorify Ulbricht as a symbol of the system. The trouble is, Ulbricht has an Achilles' heel. He wants love and esteem, but there is little in his person and policies on which public relations can feed. Moreover, the German Communists are so crude, they exaggerate so much, that their panegyrics produce the exact opposite of what they hoped for, i.e., revulsion.

Ulbricht's Policy in the 1960's

On October 4, 1960, the D.D.R. parliament met in East Berlin for its fifteenth session. *Neues Deutschland* reported that "an extraordinary event" was about to take place in that "high chamber": The Chairman of the newly founded Council of State would deliver a major address. Ulbricht spoke for several hours that day—about "the historic role of the D.D.R.," "the creative power of the people," and "human relations in the Socialist Democracy." He emphasized how important it was for the government to have close ties with its people and learn from them. But Ulbricht seemed to have forgotten a phrase he had used very frequently in Stalin's time when discussing domestic policy: *class struggle.* He talked of the "people's common interests," of the increasing participation by all citizens in the making of policy, of the true justice being realized in the state, of humanism and the spirit of community, of respect and love for man. He promised that life would become "richer and more beautiful. . . . We shall prove to all people in West Germany that Socialism is the better, more humane social system."[11]

East Germans had little reason to trust this talk about justice and humanity after what they had witnessed in the preceding months. In less than ten weeks—from February to April, 1960—the remaining independent farmers in central Germany had been brutally collectivized. It is hard to determine whether any given measure taken in East Germany originates in Moscow or East Berlin; but in this case we know that Ulbricht himself took the initiative and is personally to blame for the consequences.

At the close of 1959, independent farmers were still working 50 per cent of the tilled soil of East Germany. And even though SED functionaries were doing their best in 1958 and 1959 to get the farmers to join the Agricultural Production Cooperatives, no one expected a *blitzkrieg* on the matter. There seemed to be agreement that collectivization would be completed at the end of the Seven-Year Plan—i.e., in 1965.

Then, an agricultural conference of representatives from all the Eastern-bloc countries was held in Moscow on February 2, 1960. They agreed that something had to be done to solve the agricultural crisis, but differed over what was the speediest and most effective way to accomplish this. Khrushchev left the decision to the leaders of each country. Gomulka saw no reason to change his agricultural policy—which was based on the application of greater pressure on the private peasant economy that embraced 85 per cent of Polish agriculture. But Ulbricht decided on forced collectivization in the briefest possible time, and is supposed to have said that collectivized agriculture was the only form that could guarantee greater yields. Khrushchev and other Communist leaders agreed, in spite of the failures in Communist agricultural policy, for they could not conceive of Socialism without collectivized property in the villages. But wide differences of opinion—among SED leaders as well—remained on the tempo at which collectivization should be carried out.

The campaign against the East German farmers began when Ulbricht returned from Moscow. Some district secretaries, supported by doubters in the Party high command, warned against rash measures for fear of peasant resistance; others had no idea of what was afoot. Ulbricht, however, created a small operational group and came to an agreement with the Rostock district secretary, Karl Mewis, to conduct the first experiment in Mecklenburg. Ulbricht cautiously refrained from making any public statements while Party functionaries, FDJ groups, and the police drove the Mecklenburg farmers into the collective farms. But in talking to department heads in the Central Committee, Ulbricht explained that the peasants had to be treated like small children who did not know what was good for them and, if necessary, had to be forced into the collective farms for their own benefit. In one district after the other, the farmers had to give in to the Party workers. On April 15, the last district, Karl-Marx-Stadt (formerly Chemnitz), reported that collectivization had been completed.

Ulbricht and his Party hacks imposed collectivization by force and terror. Did he wish to dissociate himself from such methods and reassure the population after the last bastion of the bourgeoisie in the D.D.R. had fallen? The behavior of his functionaries in the autumn of 1961, a year after his declaration, destroyed any such hopes. Terror ruled the D.D.R. again in the months following the erection of the Wall on August 13. People who openly criticized the Wall were assaulted bodily by SED and Security Police shock troops; many were arrested and disappeared into the over-crowded jails and prisons. Simultaneously, meetings of factory workers and the general population were called in all towns and villages at which the helpless and desperate citizenry were compelled to "welcome" the erection of the Wall. On August 24, 1961, the Council of Ministers issued a decree—still in effect—"restricting the right of residence," which introduced forced labor and exile in the "first German Workers' and Peasants' State." A person who is found guilty of "endangering public safety and order" by his conduct can be ordered to move his residence from one locality to another, and be assigned to a job. (This is aside and apart from any sentence he may have received.) The guards on the Wall and at the frontiers of the D.D.R. received orders to shoot anyone fleeing East Germany. Scores of persons have been killed while trying to escape over cement walls, through barbed-wire entanglements, and across mined fields. Many have gone to prison for attempted escapes.

It is hard for anyone on the outside to imagine how unbearable life has become for East Germans in the months since August 13, 1961. Many have quarreled with themselves and their families because they had entertained the idea of going to the West but had been reluctant to leave their native regions, their kin, their friends, their jobs, their homes, and everything they had worked so hard to build up. Now the road to the West has been cut off, and the people suffer deeply from the knowledge that they are at the mercy of their regime. Separation from relatives living in the Federal Republic and West Berlin seems final. Most unbearable of all was the triumph of the SED enthusiasts—those who barely waited for one word of criticism before striking out and showing their power; who were not satisfied when people kept a fearful silence but demanded overt approval of the Wall, testimonials of devotion to the State Council Chairman, and self-imposed pledges to increase production. Stalin had been dead ten years, much had changed in the Eastern bloc, yet Stalinism continued its reign of terror in Germany.

Ulbricht could no longer expect the population to ascribe any real meaning to his relatively moderate-sounding speeches, such as the one he gave on June 17, 1962. Nevertheless, it was true that a change became discernible beginning about the middle of 1962. Totalitarianism in the D.D.R. is slowly losing the absolute form it reached at the end of the Stalin era. Ulbricht, too, is furtively trying to de-Stalinize the Communist system in Germany "from above," primarily in order to modernize it.

For decades, Ulbricht was considered an incorrigible Stalinist. Can a seventy-year-old man change? There is no need for him to do so. His Communism has always been essentially a reflection of Soviet Communism. Once he realized, if belatedly, that Stalin was really dead, he began to alter his attitudes. He had done this many times before, but now he possessed enough political self-confidence to change course without slavishly imitating his masters.

Ulbricht believed that the D.D.R. was not ready for the Soviet reforms and de-Stalinization, and, therefore, that these measures could not be applied. First, conditions conducive to a change in the method of rule had to be created. Socialization had to be completed and the frontiers barred; only then would the people accept that there were no alternatives outside of Communism, outside the borders of this Germany. But once collectivization was completed and the frontiers locked, Ulbricht could no longer excuse his economic and political failures by blaming them on open borders or "capitalist survivals." A few months after the Wall was built, he began systematically to apply Khrushchev's general policy in the D.D.R. But Ulbricht did not merely copy it—he put his own stamp on it.

For Ulbricht as for the Kremlin, reforms cannot be carried to the point where they threaten prevailing power relationships: The Party's power must not be undermined. Ulbricht is far more intent than Khrushchev was on suppressing any "discussion of errors." He pursues a silent, undemonstrative de-Stalinization whose primary goal is to modernize the economy, and for two reasons. First, a modernized economy, producing more and better goods, will raise East Germany's living standard. Ulbricht sees this as an important condition for reconciling the population to the government. Besides, their willingness to support and cooperate with the system is greater than before. Success here would help to improve the status of the German Democratic Republic both inside and outside the Eastern bloc. Secondly, developments since Stalin's death seem to prove that experiments and changes in the economy are relatively harmless to the stability of Communist rule; on the other hand, a slackening of the reins in cultural policy or ideology may lead to trouble and is dangerous for the Party. This may explain why Ulbricht has concentrated on economic affairs. He has acquired a great deal of knowledge in the last fifteen years and does not feel out of place in this field. He is unquestionably the driving force behind economic reforms in the D.D.R.

Under the slogan "New Economic System of Planning and Management," Ulbricht and his followers have been moving away from the principles of Stalinist economic policy since the Sixth SED Congress in January, 1963. He now condemns this policy for its bureaucratization, overcentralization, and "great mistrust of the capabilities . . . of the popular masses." Experiments and reforms are now aimed primarily at squeezing as much bureaucratic water out of the planned economy as possible, decentralizing it, and incorporating pragmatic regulators in the system. Of course, initial steps in this direction were taken more than once in the past, and with no great success. Ulbricht, other SED functionaries, and the men who run the economy now base themselves on the ideas of the Soviet economist Professor Liberman, and—without saying so—on the proposals developed in 1956–57 by East Berlin experts like Professor Behrens and Dr. Arne Benary. At the time, these men were denounced as dangerous revisionists and have still not been publicly rehabilitated.

In the new economic dispensation, the eighty combines or associations of state-owned plants, as well as individual state-owned ones, are to enjoy more rights and a certain degree of financial independence. The National Economic Council in East Berlin will set production goals; how they are fulfilled will be left largely to the plants themselves. Their work will no longer be judged in terms of rigid compliance with directives and instructions from the central economic agency, but by measurable economic and financial results. To make this possible, "economic levers" are to be incorporated in the Communist planned economy—i.e., modern economic principles such as are followed in a free economy. Earnings and profits are to be the decisive criteria.[12]

If the guided economy is to give way to a successful, businesslike one, the SED can no longer use devoted Party bureaucrats whose only ambition is to execute mindlessly the orders from the top. It needs managers who enjoy responsibility, know their field, and are willing to show initiative. "It is quite clear," Ulbricht stated in February, 1964, "that we can do without the routine administrative types in the organs of the National Economic Council, at the head of the [factories]. We must develop personnel who are genuine directors of the Socialist economy—highly qualified men thoroughly versed in the economic and technical aspects of their field, responsible, creative, and bold, distinguished by professional objectivity, sober calculation, and iron work discipline."[13] Until now, however, people with these traits have been sent to prison in the D.D.R.

There is another important aspect to the new economic policy. The workers must cooperate energetically. They will do so when material incentives in the factories are increased, when a relatively "soft" course in domestic policy is instituted. Ulbricht and other SED leaders often admit that people cannot be put off forever with mere promises of a happy future but want to live decently in the present; the masses are tired of regimentation and harassment. Party workers must show patience and understanding toward unhappy and "politically backward" elements.[14] But from all accounts, the population is skeptical about the new economic policy and its promises. Resistance was inevitable toward it and toward the changes it is producing. The main center of resistance is found among the functionaries who helped Ulbricht to Bolshevize East Germany. Now he says they accomplished "great things for the Party" but are incapable at present of overcoming "outworn methods of work and certain obsolete ideas on economic problems."

Workers on the State Planning Commission and the National Economic Council whose authority has been reduced are anxious about their influence and their future. Top economic bureaucrats now have to worry about being exiled from their privileged positions in East Berlin to minor posts in the provinces. Party officers who have only barely learned their job are being ordered to "command" and "convince." If they fail, they are open to criticism as "sectarians" and "dogmatists." Ulbricht supports the managerial élite in the conflict between the technocrats and industrial directors on the one side and the Party and administrative workers on the other. He has even brought some of the former—Dr. Erich

Apel, Dr. Günter Mittag, and Werner Jarowinsky—into the Politburo.

Ulbricht has tried as hard as he can to adapt himself to the "new times"; he has always attempted to follow the prevailing line. To everyone's surprise, he has even "survived" Khrushchev, and has seen no reason to alter his policies since the change in the Kremlin occurred. It is probable that old age, illness, or death will depose him, not an edict from the Kremlin or a palace revolution. As his life wanes, does he know that next to Stalin, he has done the most to discredit Communism in Germany? Does he know that de-Stalinization in Germany will be credible only when he is gone?

Notes

Chapter I: The Young Marxist

1. Two Ulbricht biographies have been published in East Germany. The first is the work of a well-known writer and Minister of Cultural Affairs of the German Democratic Republic (D.D.R.), Johannes R. Becher, who died in 1958: *Walter Ulbricht—Ein deutscher Arbeitersohn (Walter Ulbricht—A German Worker's Son)*. The second is written jointly by the journalist Lieselotte Thoms and Ulbricht's secretary, Hans Vieillard: *Ein guter Deutscher—Walter Ulbricht—eine biographische Skizze aus seinem Leben (A Good German, Walter Ulbricht: A Biographical Sketch of his Life)*. In addition, numerous magazine and newspaper articles on Ulbricht's life have been published in the D.D.R.

2. "Stern sprach mit der Schwester Ulbrichts" ("*Stern* Talks with Ulbricht's Sister"), *Stern*, No. 45, 1961, p. 44.

3. *Ibid.*

4. Otto Gotsche, "Studium der Arbeiterjugend damals und heute" ("Subjects Studied by Working-class Youth, Then and Now"), in *Karl-Marx-Universität, Leipzig, 1409–1959, Beiträge zur Universitätsgeschichte (Contributions to University History), Vol. II.*

5. *Ibid.*

6. *Ibid.*, and Becher, *op. cit.*, pp. 25–34.

7. Cited in Hermann Heidigger, *Die deutsche Sozialdemokratie und der nationale Staat, 1870–1920 (German Social Democracy and the National State, 1870–1920)* (Göttingen, 1956).

Chapter II: The Apparatchik

1. Thoms and Vieillard, *op. cit.*, p. 19.

2. *Rote Fahne*, February 2, 1923.

3. Ulbricht, "Vergangenheit und Zukunft der deutschen Arbeiter-bewegung" ("The Past and Future of the German Labor Movement"), report to the second plenary meeting of the Central Committee of the Socialist Unity Party (SED), *Neues Deutschland*, April 14, 1963.

4. Otto Grotewohl et al., in honor of Ulbricht's sixty-fifth birthday, *ibid.*, June 30, 1958.

5. Ulbricht's activity in Vienna has been traced in detail by Hermann Weber. The preceding description is taken from his account in *Ulbricht fälscht Geschichte: Ein Kommentar mit Dokumenten zum "Grundriss der Geschichte der deutschen Arbeiterbewegung" (Ulbricht Falsifies History)* (Cologne, 1964).

6. Ulbricht, "Jede Fabrik soll unsere Burg sein" ("Let Every Factory be our Fortress"), *Rote Fahne*, May 16, 1923; and *Inprecor*, No. 130, 1925. The article in *Rote Fahne* was later published in Ulbricht's book *Zu Fragen der Parteiarbeit (Problems of Party Work)* (East Berlin, 1960), pp., 12 ff. However, the phrase, "the struggle for a Soviet dictator-ship" was altered in the later edition to read "the struggle for power." A host of similar falsifications can be found in the East Berlin editions of Ulbricht's collected articles and speeches.

7. *Inprecor*, No. 4, 1925.

8. Ulbricht, "Mehr Planmässigkeit der Arbeit" ("More Planning in Our Work"), *ibid.*, No. 117, 1925.

9. Ulbricht, "Zur Methode der Reorganisation auf der Basis der Be-triebszellen" ("Methods of Reorganization on the Basis of Factory Cells"), *Kommunistische Internationale*, No. 8, 1925; and "Aktions-fähigkeit, Zentralismus und Disziplin" ("The Ability to Act, Centralism, and Discipline"), *Rote Fahne*, June 10, 1923.

10. Ulbricht, "Lehren und Aufgaben" ("Lessons and Tasks"), *Kom-munistische Internationale*, Nos. 34–35, 1929.

11. Ulbricht, "Der Parteitag der Kommunistischen Partei Deutsch-lands" ("The KPD Party Congress"), *ibid.*, No. 26, 1929. Ulbricht de-leted this particular passage when his speeches were prepared for a collected edition.

12. J. V. Stalin, "On the International Situation," *Bolshevik*, Septem-ber 20, 1924, and *Works* (13 vols.; Moscow: Foreign Languages Publish-ing House, 1952–55), VI, 295.

13. Ulbricht, Reichstag speeches, June 27 and December 11, 1930; March 24, 1931; and February 23, 1932.

14. Ulbricht, "Lehren und Aufgaben."

15. Ulbricht, Reichstag speech, February 23, 1932.

16. Siegfried Bahne, "Die Kommunistische Partei Deutschlands," in

Erich Matthias and Rudolf Morsey, *Das Ende der Parteien, 1933* (Düsseldorf, 1960), pp. 655 ff.; and Herbert Wehner, *Erinnerungen (Notebooks)* (mimeographed). On the results of the referendum, see Ossip K. Flechtheim, *Die KPD in der Weimarer Republik* (Offenbach, 1948), p. 176.

17. *Rote Fahne*, July 29, 1932.

18. *Loc. cit.*

Chapter III: The Survivor

1. From a letter to the editors of *Stern*.

2. "Walter" [Ulbricht], "Das kapitalistische Rettungsprogramm der SPD und die Rolle der 'Linken'" ("The SPD's Program for Saving Capitalism and the Role of the 'Left' "), *Kommunistische Internationale*, No. 12, 1934.

3. "Walter" [Ulbricht], "Organisatorische Fragen der Massenarbeit der KPD" ("Organizational Problems of the KPD's Mass Work"), Part I, *Rundschau*, No. 44, 1933; Part II, *Rundschau*, No. 46, 1933.

4. Ulbricht, "Das kapitalistische Rettungsprogramm der SPD."

5. See Franz Borkenau, *European Communism* (New York: Harper & Brothers; London: Faber and Faber, 1953), pp. 115 ff.; Günther Nollau, *International Communism and World Revolution* (New York: Praeger; London: Hollis and Carter, 1961), pp. 115 ff.; and Bahne, *op. cit.*

6. Letter, republished in *Beiträge zur Geschichte der deutschen Arbeiterbewegung*, No. 2, 1963, pp. 282 ff.

7. *Kommunistische Internationale*, No. 8, 1935.

8. Gustav Regler, *The Owl of Minerva* (New York: Farrar, Straus, and Cudahy; London: Rupert Hart Davies, 1959), p. 176.

9. Ulbricht, speech of August 7, 1935, in *Rundschau*, No. 36, 1935.

10. "Walter" [Ulbricht], "Um die Einheitsfront in Deutschland" ("On the United Front in Germany"), *Kommunistische Internationale*, No. 3, 1936. Ulbricht's letter to the SPD Executive Committee of November 10, 1935, is misquoted in this article.

11. I should like to call attention to the extremely interesting article by Babette L. Gross, Münzenberg's widow, "Die Volksfrontpolitik in den dreissiger Jahren" ("The Popular Front Policy in the 1930's"), supplement to *Das Parlament*, October 24, 1962.

12. Alfred Kantorowicz has kindly placed the complete text of this letter at my disposal. The paragraph quoted here is also quoted in his *Deutsches Tagebuch* (Munich, 1959), I, 48.

13. *Ibid.*, p. 328.

14. Ulbricht, "Fünf Jahre Hitler-herrschaft—wie kämpft das anti-faschistische Deutschland?" ("Five Years of Hitler's Rule: How is Anti-Fascist Germany Fighting?"), *Rundschau*, No. 4, 1938.

15. See Margarete Buber-Neumann, *Von Potsdam nach Moskau* (Stuttgart, 1957), p. 284.

16. *Kommunistische Internationale*, No. 5, 1937.

17. *Rundschau*, No. 26 and No. 29, 1939.

18. See Erich Wollenberg, "Der Apparat—Stalins Fünfte Kolonne" ("The *Apparat:* Stalin's Fifth Column"), *Ostprobleme*, No. 19, 1951; and Nollau, *op. cit.*, pp. 193–94.

19. Ulbricht, "Ernst Thälmann und der Freiheitskampf des deutschen Volkes" ("Ernst Thälmann and the Freedom Fight of the German People"), *Kommunistische Internationale*, No. 3, 1939.

20. "Die internationale Bedeutung des antifaschistischen Kampfes in Deutschland" ("The Meaning of the Anti-Fascist Struggle in Germany"), *Kommunistische Internationale*, No. 6, 1939.

21. Wolfgang Leonhard, *Child of the Revolution* (Chicago: Henry Regnery; London: Collins, 1958), p. 108.

22. Thoms and Vieillard, *Ein guter Deutscher*, pp. 51–52.

23. Heinrich Graf von Einsiedel, *Tagebuch der Versuchung (Diary of Temptation)* (Berlin, Stuttgart: 1950), p. 54.

24. Jesco von Puttkammer, an officer who joined the National Committee, thought that the founding meeting was a "mixture of a patriotic citizens' meeting and a Marxist Party debate." *Irrtum und Schuld—Geschichte des Nationalkomitees 'Freies Deutschland' (Error and Guilt: History of the National Committee for Free Germany)* (Berlin: 1948), p. 43.

25. Weinert later wrote the official Party account of the activities of the National Committee for Free Germany, *Das Nationalkomitee 'Freies Deutschland'—1943–1945—Bericht über seine Tätigkeit und seine Auswirkung (The National Committee for Free Germany, 1943–1945: A Report on Its Activity and Effect)* (East Berlin, 1957).

26. Leonhard, *op. cit.*, pp. 307 ff.; and Scheurig, *Freies Deutschland—Das Nationalkomitee und der Bund Deutscher Offiziere in der Sowjetunion, 1943–1945 (Free Germany: The National Committee and the League of German Officers in the Soviet Union)* (Munich: 1960), pp. 82–83.

27. Einsiedel, *op. cit.*, p. 65.

28. Thoms and Vieillard, *op. cit.*, p. 60.

29. Ulbricht, "Von der Sowjetunion lernen, heisst—siegen lernen" ("Learning from the Soviet Union Means—Learning to Conquer"),

speech on the thirty-fourth anniversary of the October Revolution, *Neues Deutschland*, November 7, 1951.

Chapter IV: The Deputy

1. Cited in Leonhard, *op. cit.*, p. 303.

2. Ulbricht, "Um die Einheit der Arbeiterklasse" ("On Working-Class Unity"), *Kommunistische Internationale*, No. 12, 1938.

3. *Einheitsfront der antifaschistisch-demokratischen Parteien (United Front of Anti-Fascist–Democratic Parties)*, pamphlet; and Ulbricht, *Zur Geschichte der neuesten Zeit (History of the Recent Past)* (East Berlin: 1955), I, 126.

4. *Dokumente zur parteipolitischen Entwicklung in Deutschland seit 1945 (Documents on the Development of Political Parties in Germany since 1945)*, pp. 313 ff.

5. Ulbricht, "Was wird aus Deutschland?" ("What Prospects for Germany?"), *Rundschau*, No. 43, 1939.

6. From a speech delivered in Munich on July 28, 1946, in Ulbricht, *Zur Geschichte der deutschen Arbeiterbewegung*, III, 22 ff.

7. See Ulbricht, "Thesen über das Wesen des Hitlerfaschismus" ("Theses on the Nature of Hitler Fascism"), *ibid.*, II, 402 ff.

8. Thoms and Vieillard, *Ein guter Deutscher*, pp. 74–75.

9. Ulbricht, "Offene Antwort an die Christlich-Demokratische Union" ("Open Answer to the Christian Democratic Union"), *Freiheit* (Halle), October 7, 1946. Reprinted in *Zur Geschichte der deutschen Arbeiterbewegung*, III, 44 ff.

10. Ulbricht, interview with a journalist, "Klärung bedeutet Festigung des Blokkes der antifaschistisch-demokratischen Parteien" ("Clarification Strengthens the Bloc of Anti-Fascist–Democratic Parties"), *Neues Deutschland*, February 1, 1950.

11. According to Erich W. Gniffke, a member of the SED Central Secretariat who fled to West Germany via West Berlin in October, 1948. He is my major source of information on power relations within the SED leadership before 1948.

12. Dennis Newson, "Forgotten Wife of Ulbricht," *Daily Herald* (London), September 18, 1962.

13. See "Kaffeestunde mit Lotte Ulbricht" ("Coffee Time with Lotte Ulbricht"), *Berliner Zeitung*, March 19, 1961.

14. Harry Prauss, *doch es war nicht die Wahrheit (But it wasn't the Truth)* (Berlin, 1960), p. 88.

15. Leonhard, "Der Ulbricht, den ich kannte" ("The Ulbricht I Knew"), *Die Zeit* (Hamburg), June 28, 1963.

Chapter V: Crises

1. *Neues Deutschland,* April 16, 1953.

2. Schenk, *op. cit.,* p. 186.

3. *Ibid.,* p. 192.

4. *Neues Deutschland,* June 17, 1953.

5. Über die Lage und die unmittelbaren Aufgaben der Partei" ("On the Situation and the Immediate Tasks of the Party"), in *Dokumente der Sozialistischen Einheitspartei Deutschlands (Documents of the SED)* (8 vols.; East Berlin, 1948–62), IV, 438 ff.

6. *Protokoll des IV. Parteitages der SED (Protocol of the Fourth SED Congress)* (East Berlin, 1954), I, 218 ff.

7. *Das 15. Plenum des Zentralkomitees der SED—Parteiinternes Material (The Fifteenth Plenary Meeting of the SED Central Committee)* (brochure of the SED, Berlin, 1953), p. 76.

8. "Der Neue Kurs und die Aufgaben der Partei" ("The New Course and the Tasks of the Party"), *Neues Deutschland,* July 28, 1953.

9. Schenk, *op. cit.,* p. 226, and Ulbricht, "Die Sowjetunion—die Bastion des Friedens, der Demokratie und des Sozialismus" ("The Soviet Union—Bastion of Peace, Democracy, and Socialism"), *Für dauerhaften Frieden, für Volksdemokratie,* No. 45, 1954.

10. Ulbricht, "Der Weg zu Frieden, Einheit und Wohlstand," ("The Road to Peace, Unity, and Prosperity"), report delivered at the sixteenth plenary meeting of the SED Central Committee (Berlin, 1953), pp. 81 ff.

11. "Das nationale Programm und seine Wirking" ("The National Program and Its Consequences"), *Tägliche Rundschau,* June 13, 1954.

12. Ulbricht, "Die Warschauer Konferenz und die neuen Aufgaben in Deutschland" ("The Warsaw Conference and the New Tasks in Germany"), speech delivered at the twenty-fourth plenary meeting of the SED Central Committee, June 1–2, 1955.

13. Ulbricht, answer to questions raised at the SED Conference of Berlin District Delegates, *Neues Deutschland,* March 18, 1956.

14. See *Protokoll des II. Parteitages der SED (Protocol of the Second SED Congress)* (East Berlin, 1952).

15. See Ulbricht, "Zu einigen Problemen der III. Parteikonferenz—Aus dem Referat auf der Beratung des Parteiaktivs der SED, Bezirk Leipzig" ("On Some Problems of the Third Party Conference—From the Report on the Discussion of Leipzig District Party Activists"), April 5, 1956, in *Zur Geschichte der deutschen Arbeiterbewegung,* VI, 10.

16. *"Über die Arbeit der SED nach dem XX. Parteitag der KPDSU und die bisherige Durchführung der Beschlüsse der 3. Parteikonferenz"*

("On the Work of the SED Since the Twentieth Party Congress of the CPSU and the Execution of the Decisions of the Third Party Conference"), report delivered at the twenty-eighth meeting of the SED Central Committee, July 27–29, 1956 (Berlin, 1956), pp. 29, 45.

17. See Ulbricht, "Zur wissenschaftlichen Diskussion an den Universitäten" ("Scientific Discussion in the Universities"), a speech to SED Party activists at Humboldt University, *Zur Geschichte der deutschen Areiterbewegung*, VI, 65 ff.

18. See Ulbricht's speech at the thirteenth plenum of the SED Central Committee, *ibid.*, VI, 325.

19. Schenk, *op. cit.*, pp. 306 ff.

Chapter VI: Ulbricht and Communist Policy on Germany

1. Excerpts reprinted in *Neues Deutschland*, March 18, 1950.

2. *Protokoll des III. Parteitages der SED*, pp. 412 ff.

3. See Ulbricht, "Von der Sowjetunion lernen heisst—siegen lernen," and "Das grosse Programm des Kampfes und des Sieges" ("The Great Program of Struggle and Victory"), *Neues Deutschland*, October 23, 1952.

4. See "Georgi Dimitroffs Vermächtnis: Die Aktionseinheit schaffen" ("Georgi Dimitroff's Legacy: To Create Unity of Action"), *Neues Deutschland*, June 19, 1952.

5. See "Das Wiedererstehen des deutschen Imperialismus" ("The Resurrection of German Imperialism"), *Einheit*, No. 10, 1951.

6. See Ulbricht, New Year's speeches for 1956 and 1957, *Zur Geschichte der deutschen Arbeiterbewegung*, V, 203, and VI, 262; speech at the twenty-fourth plenary meeting of the SED Central Committee, June, 1955 (Berlin, 1955), p. 28; Protokoll der 3. Parteikonferenz der SED (Protocol of the Third SED Conference), pp. 47 ff; closing speech at the Conference on Improving Party Working Methods, December, 1957, *Zur Geschichte der deutschen Arbeiterbewegung*, VII, 26 ff; speech at the thirty-third plenary meeting of the SED Central Committee, October, 1957 (unpublished account of proceedings); speech to the East German Parliament, February 10, 1958, *Zur Geschichte der deutschen Arbeiterbewegung*, VII, 107 ff.; "Jahre der Wende" ("Year of the Turning-point"), *Neues Deutschland*, January 1, 1959; and *Protokoll des VI. Parteitages der SED* (Protocol of the Sixth Party Congress of the SED), I, 58.

7. See Beate Ruhm von Oppen, ed., *Documents on Germany Under Occupation*, 1945–1954 (New York: Oxford University Press, 1955).

8. Ulbricht, "Antwort an sozialdemokratische funktionäre" ("Reply

to Social Democratic Functionaries"), *Neues Deutschland*, November 26, 1955.

9. Ulbricht, "Grundfragen der Politik der SED" ("Basic Questions of SED Policy"), *Neues Deutschland*, February 3, 1957; speech at the thirty-third plenum of the SED Central Committee, October, 1957; interview with Kempski, chief correspondent of the *Süddeutsche Zeitung*, reprinted in *Neues Deutschland*, February 16, 1948; "Die Staatslehre des Marxismus-Leninismus und ihre Anwendung in Deutschland" ("Marxist-Leninist Political Theory and Its Application in Germany"), April, 1958. Ulbricht discussed the confederation plan in all these speeches or interviews.

10. Ulbricht, "Macht Berlin zur Haupstadt des Friedens!" ("Make Berlin the Peace Capital!"), speech at a meeting of Berlin Party activists, May 21, 1957, in *Neues Deutschland*, May 23, 1957.

11. Ulbricht, "An die Arbeiterschaft und alle friedliebenden Bürger Westberlins!" ("To the Workers and Peace-Loving Citizens of West Berlin!"), *Neues Deutschland*, October 28, 1958.

12. Quoted here from *Leipziger Volkszeitung*, June 16–17, 1961. The relevant paragraph on the Wall carries the subtitle "We're Not Building Any Wall."

13. Ulbricht, "Es ist allerhöchste Zeit für den Friedensvertrag" ("It's High Time to Conclude the Peace Treaty"), *Neues Deutschland*, August 11, 1961.

14. *Neues Deutschland*, October 21, 1961.

15. See *Neues Deutschland*, January 4, 1964; see also Ulbricht's interview with *Stern*, "Das offene deutsche Gespräch" ("The Open German Dialogue"), *Neues Deutschland*, November 28, 1963; excerpts published in *Stern*, No. 48, 1963.

16. See *Neues Deutschland*, January 4, 1964.

Chapter VII: The Chairman of the Council of State

1. Excerpts were published in *Der Spiegel*, No. 33, 1962, under the title "Alle haben Walter lieb" ("They All Love Walter").

2. Otto Gotsche, "Weil er unser Genosse ist" ("Because He Is Our Comrade"), *Neues Deutschland*, June 29, 1963.

3. "Wenn gute Freunde miteinander sprechen" ("When Good Friends Converse"), *Freie Presse*, January 28, 1961.

4. "Arbeitstil eines Kandidaten des Volkes" ("Working Method of a People's Candidate"), *Neues Deutschland*, September 15, 1950.

5. In *Junge Generation*, No. 23, 1961.

6. See Otto Nagel, "Wie hilft die Kunst?" ("How Does Art Help?")

in the book of essays *Walter Ulbricht,* issued in honor of Ulbricht's seventieth birthday. See also, in the same volume, Lea Grundig, "In der V. Deutschen Kunstausstellung" ("At the Fifth German Art Exhibition").

7. *Neues Deutschland,* December 8, 1961.

8. Ulbricht "Die neuen Aufgaben im nationalen Aufbau" ("The New Tasks in National Construction"), speech at the Conference on Architecture, April 3, 1955; reprinted in *Zur Geschichte der deutschen Arbeiterbewegung,* V, 262; and "Zeugnis sozialistischer Kultur" ("Evidence of Socialist Culture"), speech to the builders of the Leipzig Opera House, *Neues Deutschland,* October 11, 1960.

9. See Hermann Henselmann, "Kühnheit und Disziplin, Phantasie und Planmässigkeit" ("Daring and Discipline, Imagination and Planning"), *Sonntag,* No. 26, 1958.

10. Alexander Abusch, "Über die revolutionäre Arbeitsmethode des Genossen Walter Ulbricht" ("On the Revolutionary Work Methods of Comrade Ulbricht"), *Einheit,* No. 6, 1958.

11. Ulbricht, programmatic statement delivered before the East German Parliament, October 4, 1960, *Neues Deutschland,* October 5, 1960.

12. On relations between economic interests of individual factories and the Plan, see "Richtlinien für das neue ökonomische System der Planung und Leitung der Volkswirtschaft ("Guidelines for the New Economic System of Planning and Management in the National Economy"), supplement to *Neues Deutschland,* July 16, 1963.

13. Ulbricht, speech at the fifth plenary meeting of the SED Central Committee, *Neues Deutschland,* February 5 and 6, 1964.

14. See the revealing article, "Sektierertum—Todfeind der Massenarbeit" ("Sectarianism—Mortal Enemy of Mass Work"), *Neuer Weg,* No. 2, 1964.

Index

Abusch, Alexander, 66n
Ackermann, Anton, 65n, 92, 101, 105, 118, 143, 150, 155
Adenauer, Konrad, 179, 180, 182, 183, 185n
Allgemeine Deutsche Arbeiterverein, 4
Apel, Erich, 213–14
Arendsee, Martha, 101
Austria, 30, 31, 84; Communist Party of, 30, 31
Axen, Hermann, 125

Bauer, Otto, 23
Baum, Bruno, 144, 145
Bebel, August, 4, 9, 12
Becher, Johannes R., 24, 25, 71n, 88, 101, 202
Behrens, Friedrich, 212
Benary, Arne, 212
Benjamin, Hilde, 196
Beria, Lavrenti, 139, 142, 148, 149, 150, 184
Bernhard, Georg, 68
Bernstein, Eduard, 12
Bertz, Paul, 65n, 75n
Berzarin, Nikolai E., 98, 100
Beutling, Theodor, 78
Birkenhauer, Erich, 78
Black Front, 69n
Blum, Léon, 71
Bolz, Lothar, 89

Brandler, Heinrich, 25–26, 28, 30
Brandt, Heinz, 144
Braun, Max, 67, 68, 69
Brazil, 182n
Brecht, Bertolt, 158
Bredel, Willi, 88
Breitscheid, Rudolf, 67, 68, 69
Brüning, Heinrich, 38, 52n
Buber-Neumann, Margarete, 85n
Bulgaria, 120; Communist Party of, 60

Center Party, 38, 52n
Christian Democratic Party (CDU), 106, 113, 114
Chwalek, Roman, 100
Communist International (Comintern), 24, 27, 29–31, 35, 44, 46–47, 59–62, 64–65, 70, 71, 77, 79–82, 85, 93; First World Congress, 78; Second World Congress, 31; Third World Congress, 24; Fourth World Congress, 25; Seventh World Congress, 60, 62, 64, 65n, 66, 67
Communist Party of Germany, 16, 19, 20, 21, 23–24, 26, 27, 28, 35–36, 42–45, 57, 62n, 63, 65–66, 102–4, 119, 130; Central Committee, 25, 26–27, 61, 65, 66n, 101, 103, 108; organization, 21, 29–30, 31–35; outlawed, *1923–*